LOST CARS OF THE 1960s

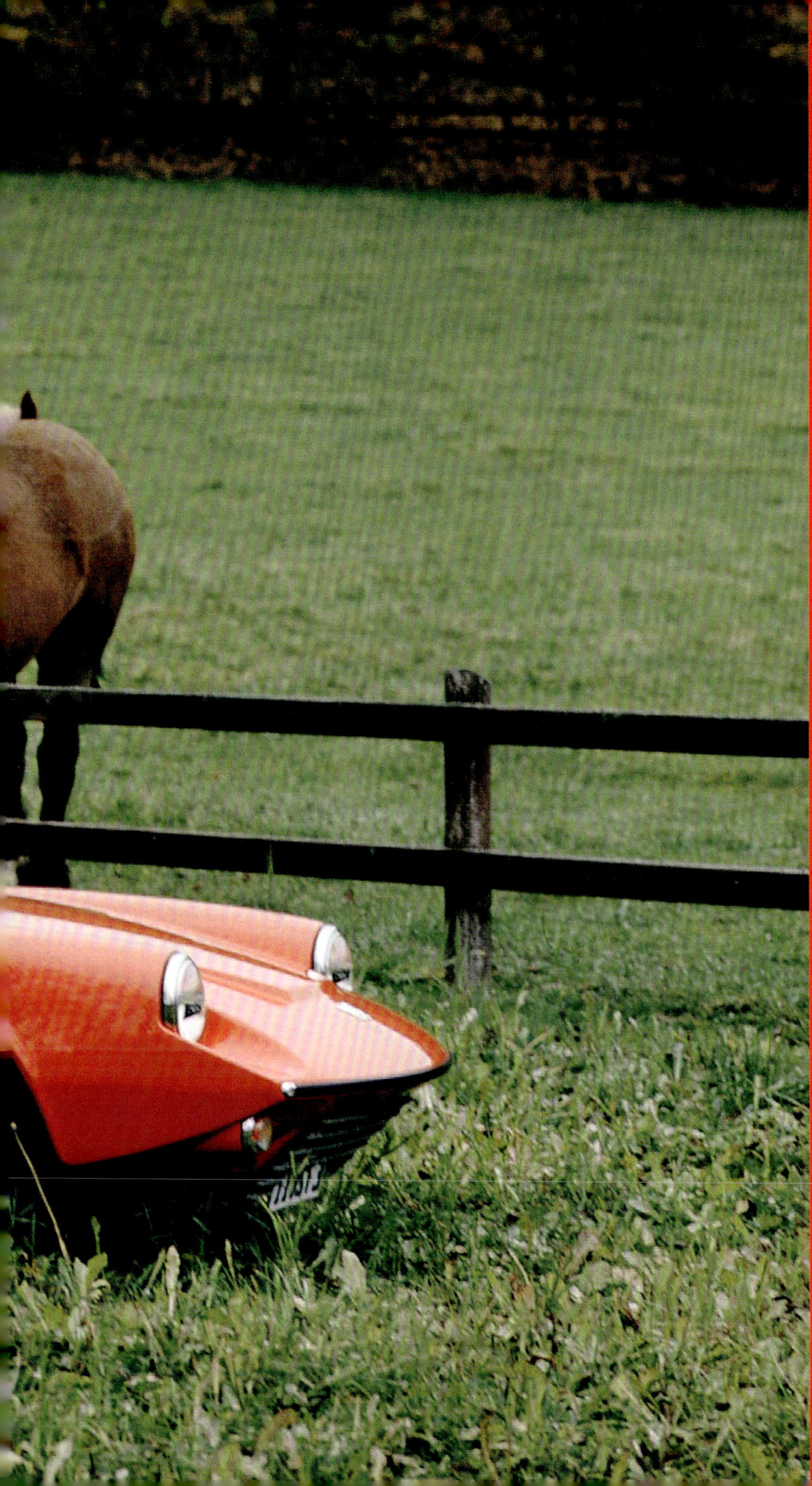

LOST CARS OF THE 1960s

GILES CHAPMAN

The History Press

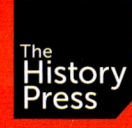

First published 2025

The History Press
97 St George's Place, Cheltenham,
Gloucestershire, GL50 3QB
www.thehistorypress.co.uk

© Giles Chapman, 2025

The right of Giles Chapman to be identified as the Author of this work has been asserted in accordance with the Copyright, Designs and Patents Act 1988.

All rights reserved. No part of this book may be reprinted or reproduced or utilised in any form or by any electronic, mechanical or other means, now known or hereafter invented, including photocopying and recording, or in any information storage or retrieval system, without the permission in writing from the Publishers.

British Library Cataloguing in Publication Data.
A catalogue record for this book is available from the British Library.

ISBN 978 1 80399 936 4

Typesetting and origination by The History Press
Printed in Turkey by Imak.

EU Authorised Representative: Easy Access System Europe
Mustamäe tee 50, 10621 Tallinn, Estonia
gpst.request@easproject.com

Front cover illustrations, clockwise from top: Daimler Majestic Major, International Harvester Scout 80, SEAT 850 Sport, Škoda 1000 MBX De Luxe.

Back cover illustration: Ford Taunus P4 12M coupé.

Previous page: Saab Sonett II.

Above: Dodge Lancer.

INTRODUCTION

This is the final book in a trilogy, filling the gap between the two others published in 2022 and 2023. Just as for *Lost Cars of the 1970s* and *Lost Cars of the 1940s & '50s*, you'll discover some of the more elusive and misunderstood cars of the 1960s. I'm sure you'll recognise several immediately, maybe do a double take at rather more, and be flummoxed by a handful. It's not a compendium of failure, more a study of what happens when circumstances conspire against best laid-plans and sometimes clever thinking. There are sixty very diverse cars here, from all over the world, along with another thirty rare showpieces and prototypes pictured to add visual richness.

The list of what to include was my first challenge; what cars are 'lost' to us in meaningful ways? The 1960s is a tricky decade for this because for most renowned marques, and many smaller ones, it's THE golden classic era, and most of these cars are too well-known to count. It took almost as long to refine that as it did to write the text and find the rare period images.

In the writing, interesting strands emerged that shaped all these cars just like their more celebrated counterparts. Technologically, it was the period when the BMC Mini's front-wheel drive/transverse engine drivetrain spread its influence rapidly, while front disc brakes and all-synchromesh gearboxes – rare in 1960 – were expected in the cheapest cars by 1970. Carmakers grappled with radical engines, abandoning gas-turbine 'jet' power and embracing the rotary engine until its economic disadvantages hit home.

The sport-utility vehicle, or SUV, roared into life, and while the USA struggled to create 'compact' cars, Japan was tackling micro-motoring in new and interesting ways. We also witnessed the controversial birth of international 'platform sharing', with the Renault 12 acting as midwife!

Mid-mounted engines transferred from racing to road cars, aiming for the ultimate in high-octane roadholding; the layout featured in many startling wedge-shaped 'dream cars' with unusual doors and cockpits. And this was the period when the gifted influence of named Italian designers Giovanni Michelotti and Giorgetto Giugiaro shaped cars you encountered all over the world. Plus, of course, trade restrictions and tariffs were still rife, resulting in unusual hybrids designed to drive round these barriers.

There's so much to unpack and comprehend in these pages, and I hope you enjoy *Lost Cars of the 1960s* as much as I have enjoyed assembling it!

ACKNOWLEDGEMENTS

A word, principally, on the pictures in this book. The vast majority originate from the manufacturers themselves. These are either as 'hard copy' prints and transparencies in the author's collection amassed over forty years; from the companies themselves via their media websites (it is amazing the efforts many go to to make this material available … although careful searching is still needed); or via the press agency Newspress. All are used in the spirit of spreading knowledge about forgotten or overlooked motor cars.

I must extend particular thanks to Mercedes-Benz for use of the image of the 600 two-door on p. 76. I'm also extremely grateful to Tim Pollard and Ben Miller at *Car* magazine for graciously allowing me to use one of their classic covers to illustrate the Lombardi 850 Grand Prix (p. 138).

Rolls-Royce and coachbuilding expert Tom Clarke helped with my understanding of the James Young Rolls-Royce Silver Shadow (p. 93), as did Adam at www.jamesyounglimited.com, who is devoted to tracking down all surviving examples.

My very dear friend and former art director Nick Kisch kindly guided me in choosing the best images from the available selection, while fellow author Russell Hayes helped me get a handle on how unusual the two-door Ford Corsair really is.

I'd like to dedicate *Lost Cars of the 1960s* to the members of our Car Nerds 'supper club': John Antonaki, Claude Berthollier, Martin Buckley, Robert Dicks, Ian Dixon-Potter, the aforementioned Nick Kisch, Michael Morrison and Stefan Szecsei. The kind of stuff in this book and in the other two in the trilogy is what we tend to indulge in over wine and food. Long may we bang on, although sadly no longer with Nick, who passed away before this book went to press. So it is especially dedicated to him.

Left: Autobianchi Primula.

Above: A windscreen bug deflector helps wind-cheating Giulia SS drivers.

Right: An original Giulietta SS; the most exciting car on the road pre-Jaguar E-type.

1960 ALFA ROMEO GIULIETTA & GIULIA SPRINT SPECIALE

We begin our journey through the twisting, distant roadscape of the 1960s with a desirable coupé that always begged to be driven but, as one of the rarest Alfa Romeos of the whole decade, was denied almost everyone bar a select band of wealthy sportsmen.

This Sprint Speciale (SS) was the culmination of everything that Carrozzeria Bertone could offer its most important client, Alfa Romeo. The Milan-based manufacturer had already bestowed it with a valuable contract to build the Giulietta Sprint coupé body, but now company owner Nuccio Bertone pitched for more with a daring GT mainly intended to win races.

It began with a ground-hugging prototype in 1957 shaped by Franco Scaglione, his chief stylist. Scaglione was responsible for the regular Sprint and also a series of three *Berlina Aerodinamica Tecnica* experimental vehicles – the famous 'BAT' cars – intended to explore how far practicality might be combined with wind-cheating lines. And the SS certainly did have incredible aerodynamics, with a co-efficient of drag of a mere 0.28; even today that's considered very 'slippery'.

The first 100 production SS cars stuck to the original low-nose outline because this run was to homologate it for international motor sport. A handful even had super-light aluminium coachwork, and they're now highly prized. The Giulietta engine was a hot 100bhp version of the regular 1.2-litre, double-overhead-camshaft, four-cylinder, with twin Weber carburettors. Its power and the car's superb streamlining made it capable of an astonishing 124mph, and a five-speed gearbox was part of the driver-focused package.

With stripped-out interior and Plexiglass windows, this Giulietta SS was just too raw for most, so Bertone's regular edition has a raised nose, slim bumpers, and a more comfortable interior with extra soundproofing. The looks were unsullied, though, and in a time just before the Jaguar E-type the SS was the most sensational-looking new car on the road: fast, furious, scarce and beautiful.

In 1962, and after just 1,366 of these exotic machines had been delivered, the SS was upgraded after the Giulietta series was replaced by the Giulia range. The chief difference was a 1.6-litre twin-cam, now with 113bhp on tap, and low-revs/high-torque characteristics encouraging spirited driving. The coveted SS barely changed externally, apart from a leather-covered dashboard instead of a painted metal one. After the 200th car was completed, disc brakes arrived for the front wheels, not a moment too soon for this eager race winner.

Once again, these cars were like hen's teeth. Just 1,400 Giulia SSs were made. This time, British buyers didn't have to put up with a driver's seat on the wrong side, as tuning firm Ruddspeed converted a batch of twenty-five Giulia 1600 SSs to right-hand drive. Despite being 75kg (165lb) heavier than the Giulietta SS, the Giulia 1600 SS reached a top speed of 118mph, and competition achievements included the Consuma and Stallavena-Boscochiesanuova hill climbs, the 1967–70 Targa Florio, and endurance races at Monza in the Coppa Intereuropa, at Mugello, and even at the 24 Hours of Daytona in 1969.

Above: Traditional lines belied the rapid performance car within.

Opposite: The Majestic Major limousine was usually found outside churches and town halls.

1960 DAIMLER MAJESTIC MAJOR

The transformation of the Daimler Majestic into the Majestic Major was a dramatic rescue job that owed much, believe it or not, to motorcycle technology. This was in essence a heart transplant. Out came the Majestic's heavy, ineffective, 3.8-litre straight-six and in went an all-new 4.5-litre V8. Its aluminium head featured hemispherical combustion chambers, whose internal profile generated more pressure and so abundant power. It had 220bhp on tap compared to the Majestic's 147bhp, while maximum torque similarly snowballed from 209lb ft at 2,900rpm to 283 at 3,200rpm.

This V8 was designed by Edward Turner, an engineer who'd forged his reputation perfecting power units with hemi-heads for Triumph motorbikes, and who throughout the late 1950s was also the managing director of Daimler and the other car and motorbike interests of the BSA group. The fact he could run the business *and* design great engines made him a unique character in the British motor industry, hence the blue plaque today on the modest house in Peckham, south-east London, where he hailed from.

Radical change had been necessary because the Daimler Majestic, introduced in 1958, was being hammered by the Jaguar MkIX, and increasingly by imported Mercedes-Benzs too, in the UK market. It was deeply old-fashioned, with a massive separate chassis that had its roots in the 1930s, slab-sided and upright bodywork, and the aforementioned feeble performance, which included a top speed of just 101mph. And they demanded £2,495 for one, £500 more than the MkIX. Daimler could counter that far more craftsmanship went into the coach-built body and finer materials, but the world was moving on fast.

The new Majestic Major – unveiled in October 1959 and on sale thirteen months later – now offered truly sparkling performance. It could sprint from 0–60mph in 9.7 seconds and surge on to a 122mph top speed. What's more, and despite a 6in increase in length over the Majestic to give truly cavernous boot space, the roadholding was surprisingly good – stable in crosswinds and sure-footed in corners. The servo-assisted Dunlop disc brakes on all four wheels, inherited from its predecessor, did a magnificent job, as did the Borg Warner automatic transmission, while power steering was a must-have option, standardised from 1964.

Even before the Majestic Major went on sale at £3,166, its fate was sealed. In May 1960 an expanding Jaguar bought Daimler from BSA for £3.1 million, and the following year Jaguar's own MkX arrived with sleek styling, monocoque construction, independent rear suspension, and undercutting it by 25 per cent at £2,393. In 1962 a stretch limousine Majestic Major went on sale, pitched at mayors and funeral directors and, although the cars were available until 1968, they sold in pretty tiny numbers: 1,191 standard saloons (fewer than the old Majestic at 1,400) and 867 limos, amounting on average to five cars a week. Turner's terrific engine was axed and never used in any other car. Jaguar reportedly tried one in a MkX (against which the Major was actually faster to 80mph) and coaxed 135mph from it but could see no advantage in swapping it for its own 4.2-litre straight-six XK engine.

Below: The unique Sahara bonnet cradles the spare wheel.

Opposite: A 2CV Sahara could tackle a 40-degree incline, slowly but surely.

1960 CITROËN 2CV SAHARA

It is just so hard today to get your head around the thinking that, in order to produce an extremely lightweight four-wheel drive car, you would put an extra engine in the back of a normal one. Citroën did just that, though, and for a time in the early 1960s – when Jeeps and Land Rovers were the only alternatives, and the tiny Suzuki LJ80 was still many years ahead – it sort of made sense.

This version of the 2CV shared the lovable profile of France's famous 'tin snail' but underneath it was radically altered. An especially beefed up chassis had a bulky transmission tunnel down its middle to link up both the 13.5bhp two-cylinder engines. There were two ignition keys, and two starter buttons, while a cable running from the front carburettor provided co-ordinated action with its rear-mounted counterpart. Both gearboxes were jointly operated by a floor-mounted gear lever, rather than its usual position in the dashboard, and there were twin hydraulic clutches. An additional lever allowed the driver to disengage the rear engine for front-drive only, and it was also feasible to use just the one at the back in an emergency, by holding in the front clutch.

Confused? You should be, although in action the 2CV Sahara was surprisingly effective and 'normal' and, compared to a normal 2CV, pretty sprightly. The raucous, air-cooled 425cc power units had raised compression ratios and slightly bigger carburettors than usual. Although never remotely fast, the Sahara could crawl its way up a slippery 40 per cent gradient (no road in France was that steep), and all the additional machinery on board, including the specially manufactured rear axle, added just 175kg (386lb) to its weight. Sump guards attached to the front and rear bumpers warded off boulders.

The extra engine meant some nifty hacks were needed to accommodate the essentials. Twin fuel tanks were tucked in below the front seats, with filler necks sticking out through the doors, and the spare wheel was strapped to a specially modified bonnet. Wider wheels with low-pressure tyres required cut-outs in the rear wings, with vents above to cool the back engine. And, because of that engine's position, the back seat was shifted forwards, so there was very little rear legroom.

Citroën did all of this to make a light yet unstoppable car for oil prospectors and other intrepid types operating across the French empire in north Africa, where black gold might lurk under those shifting sand dunes. The idea sprang from a one-off built in 1954 by Maurice Bonnafous, a local government surveyor from Landes, south-west France, who drove his twin-engined 4×4 2CV for 100,000km (62,137 miles) with no apparent malfunctions. Citroën heard about it through its dealer network, and asked its Panhard military vehicle division to take a look. By 1957 it had a factory prototype completed, which in March 1958 was shown to the media at Mer de Sable, a sandy spot not dissimilar to the Sahara.

Production began in December 1960, but at 10,230 Francs it was twice the price of a standard 2CV, while France's colonial power was waning rapidly. The car's name change to simply 2CV 4×4 in 1962 reflected that. It was axed in 1967 after a mere 694 had been delivered. Citroën did return to the featherlight off-roader theme in 1979 with the Mehari 4×4, but it had to get by on just one engine.

Above: Minimalist Mazda brought style to the *Kei* car.

Opposite: There are four, wafer-thin seats inside the tiny R360 coupé.

1960 MAZDA R360

From humble foundations as a Hiroshima-based cork manufacturer in 1920, Mazda aimed for the big time early on. In 1931 it started making three-wheeled motorised trucks and rickshaws, and four years later was renowned for its machine tools, particularly drills. The company hurtled towards car manufacturer and almost got there with a 1940 prototype, although all progress was doomed by the Second World War's devastation.

The atomic bomb that fell on Hiroshima sent shockwaves that blew out the windows and lifted the roof off Mazda's factory. Once the place was patched up, it got back on its feet with the Mazda Go, a basic three-wheeler that helped rebuild the Japanese economy. It took a long time to consider cars again, but when the R360 arrived in 1960 it was a carefully planned design.

Mazda intended to expand with the country's motorists and was in at the very bottom with a four-seater mini-car to entice budget-conscious early adopters. Unlike other contenders in the *Kei* segment – where cars could be no more than 3m long, 1.3m wide, 2m tall and offer an engine of 360cc or less – the 360 was a stylish little coupé capable of 70mpg.

The chic and dainty appearance was paired with a 356cc V-twin-cylinder engine, air cooled, producing a paltry 16bhp. It was noisy but because it was a four-stroke it didn't stink of unburnt fuel like a two-stroke moped. A 56mph top speed and leisurely acceleration were on offer, but this was sufficient for the urban roads of contemporary Japan. Front and rear torsion bar suspension provided adequate ride comfort; rack and pinion steering felt precise and sharp. Notable lightness was aided by a plastic rear window and aluminium bonnet. Interestingly, although a four-speed manual gearbox was provided, there was soon a two-speed semi-automatic option – only the second self-changer offered in Japan after Toyota's Toyoglide. Green, maroon or blue paintwork came as standard, and natty blue/white or red/white two-tones for the Deluxe with matching blue or red interiors, which had four wafer-thin seats inside.

The term 'instant hit' applies to the R360. Some 4,500 were ordered by its first day on sale in May 1960, and that year an impressive 23,417 examples were delivered – there were under 460,000 private cars across the entire country. This one model alone accounted for 15 per cent of the Japanese market in 1960, and more than three-fifths of its *Kei* car subdivision.

By 1962, Mazda added the P360 Carol to its repertoire, a bigger saloon with either two or four doors. The 358cc engine, now water-cooled, remains remarkable to this day as one of the very smallest four-cylinder units ever marketed. It gave R360 owners something to aspire to, and was another very strong seller. Sharing the same super-compact length as the R360, the Carol used a reverse-rake rear window, like a Ford Anglia 105E's, for added rear headroom.

Almost never seen outside Japan, the R360 rarely gets credit for seeding Mazda in the car business, and even less for being conceived as an ideal product for its time. It was manufactured until 1966.

1960 PININFARINA ALFA ROMEO 6C 3500

This was a working prototype that used an older 6C 3000 chassis and was an exercise in glass design, with its fully transparent roof flowing from the windscreen and side windows; the panes above the seats were removable … with care. Revealed in Geneva in 1960, it's seen frequently today at concours d'elegance shows.

1960 MERCEDES-BENZ 300 MEASURING CAR

Using one of the very last W189 300d models as a basis, Mercedes-Benz built this huge station wagon as a rolling laboratory to gather data from prototypes driving ahead of it; fourteen simultaneous measurements could be taken while travelling, transmitted via cables connecting the two cars as they moved in convoy.

Above: Harmonious Italian styling for the Skyline Sport, a first for any Japanese car.

Right: The regular Prince Skyline sedan was very Americanised in character.

1960 PRINCE SKYLINE SPORT

By the late 1950s Prince Motors was putting distance between itself and all its domestic rivals to become the most upmarket of Japanese marques. Its exotic Skyline Sport surely sparked jealousy at Toyota and Nissan, especially as it was unveiled not in the Japan Trade Center at the Tokyo motor show but the hushed elegance of the Salone di Torino in Italy.

The city was also home to Giovanni Michelotti, then the world's hottest freelance car stylist. His hundreds of designs during the 1950s, working often for Vignale and moulding the early supercar image of Ferrari, brought him a slow-burn fame that led to lucrative design contracts with Triumph, Alpine and BMW. When the Prince board decided they needed a premium range-topper, Michelotti was contacted and its chief engineer Shinichiro Sakurai sent to Turin to negotiate. The Skyline Sport then became the first ever Italian-designed Japanese car.

And a very distinctive one too, with its quadruple headlights in slanted pairs, expensive-looking radiator grille, crisp profile and a speed-suggestive side strake connecting the rear wheelarches and lights. This motif was found on numerous Michelotti designs and remained with successive generations of Skyline models as a characterful crease in the rear wing.

Underneath its sharp suit, the Skyline used the drivetrain of the regular Prince Skyline/Gloria, a saloon whose Americanised looks suddenly seemed rather passé. The engine was a 1862cc, overhead-valve four-cylinder, with a four-speed manual gearbox, De Dion tube rear suspension for the solid axle and MacPherson struts up front.

The bright blue Turin showpiece was probably the first Japanese vehicle to gain any international credibility. The following year a gleaming white convertible edition was shown in Tokyo, and in April 1962 Prince commenced deliveries. Only the rear-view mirror and the emblems were changed from the original show car. Giovanni Michelotti arranged for some Italian coachbuilders and panel beaters to travel to Japan to show three Prince workers how to craft each body individually by hand, and that level of bespoke build made it fantastically expensive at 1,850,000 Yen for a coupé and 1,950,000 for a convertible – at least four times the price of a typical saloon like the Datsun Bluebird. Many small parts had to be imported from Italy, swelling the cost. Consequently only sixty were made, and most Japanese people only came close to one at the cinema, after Sports featured in several movies made by Toho Studios.

The production version was not, with its 94bhp, especially quick, with a quoted top speed of 93mph. With all-drum brakes, moreover, its stopping power wasn't the best either. But the car did occasionally take to the racetrack, notably at the 1963 Nippon Grand Prix at Suzuka. The company certainly cultivated its European links: it entered a Skyline (albeit a standard four-door saloon driven by two Frenchmen, that didn't finish) in the 1962 Liège-Sofia-Liège Rally – the first ever Japanese factory team to compete in European motor sport. Prince Motors was acquired by Nissan in 1966. The Skyline was incorporated into its range and has remained there ever since.

Above: The 1961-model Lancer – here in station wagon form – was loved by buyers.

Right: The two-door hardtop Lancer GT for 1962, with pillarless side windows.

1961 DODGE LANCER

Bold or downright hideous? History has not been particularly gentle with this Dodge Lancer and the car it's derived from, the 1960-model Valiant. It seems the flattened rear fins, the unusual sculpts and folds of the bodywork flanks, and the spare wheel shape tackily pressed into the boot lid come in for plenty of retrospective scorn. It draws on bits of the 1960 Plymouth XNR show car, and that's also quite an opinion splitter. It was all the work of stylist Virgil Exner, who called it his 'Forward Look'.

The Valiant's global debut was staged at the 1959 London Motor Show in Earl's Court. To the casual observer, this appears somewhat weird because the car was never actually sold in the UK. But the European connection does illuminate the thinking around its conception. By the mid-1950s the Volkswagen Beetle was making serious inroads into the North American car market, selling so strongly that the domestic carmakers became spooked. This was the era of 20ft-long, chrome-laden land barges and a cynical 'planned obsolescence' with decorative annual updates. Yet many consumers were running in the opposite direction, picking an ugly, air-cooled economy car that changed barely at all year on year.

Detroit suddenly got a mania for 'compacts' in its fight with VW, and by 1960 all three of the big guns had their responses ready: Ford's Falcon, the Chevrolet Corvair from General Motors, and Chrysler's Valiant. The conflicted Detroit establishment seemed to overlook the reality of the Beetle's appeal – its simplicity and integrity – although the Corvair did ape its rear-engined layout.

The unspoken farce was that none of them was remotely compact by European standards. The Valiant was, at 184in long, 5in longer than a Vauxhall Cresta PA, but was still a couple of feet smaller than the biggest US sedans. With its fully monocoque construction and torsion bar front suspension, it also felt tauter and less wallowy.

In 1961 came this version of the car for Chrysler's Dodge division (Valiants were sold through Plymouth dealers). The bodywork was identical but interior and trim were a luxurious step up, with a new full-width grille and round tail-lamps … and without the fake spare wheel.

Power came from a straight-six 2.8-litre engine, slanted at 30° for a low bonnet line, with 101bhp on tap. However, a 145bhp 3.7-litre version was also available, and that could be had with a cast aluminium engine block that was 80lb lighter to improve handling and performance. With Hyper-Pak tuning kit specified, the quickest Lancer offered a fiery 196bhp, and 0–60mph acceleration in a scorching 8.6 seconds. Lancers came as two- and four-door pillarless hardtop, four-door sedan, and station wagon, with a three-speed manual or pushbutton-operated, three-speed, Torqueflite automatic.

Buyers surveyed by *Popular Mechanics* magazine said they loved their '61 Lancers, with a 77 per cent approval rating. Yet sales collapsed by more than half for the following year as the design dated in super-quick time. It was replaced by the Dodge Dart for 1963. These Lancers, the low-priced bedrock of the Dodge range, looked terrible once they got a little care-worn, with rust taking hold quickly if neglected, and survivors are pretty rare.

Above: The Contessa was the big leap forward for Hino after building Renaults.

Opposite: Air intakes behind the rear doors to ventilate the 35bhp Renault engine.

1961 HINO CONTESSA 900

Japan's early days of car making are shadowy and mysterious. Before the Second World War there were plenty of announcements and failed starts until Toyota came along in 1936. Then there was the conflict itself, from which the country emerged wrecked. The initial priority was then for trucks and buses, and as there was no background of automotive development – engineers having worked largely in aircraft and weaponry – there was no one to design any cars.

Still, in Japan's own version of the Marshall Plan for Europe, the Ministry of International Trade & Industry (MITI) and the Bank of Japan teamed up to get things going. Foreign car companies wanted to exploit the market but the government set out highly protectionist ground rules, and that meant partnering with local firms. MITI brokered the deals, and guaranteed payment for parts, establishing production lines, and royalties in dollars. Two British firms, British Motor Corporation and Rootes Group, quickly signed licence agreements, and they were hastily followed by Renault from France. The Americans were kept out – their cars were deemed unsuitably big …

In 1951, MITI lined Renault up with truck maker Hino Diesel Industry Co. Ltd just outside Tokyo, and the rear-engined Renault 4CV was selected, because there were already some of them in Japan being used as taxis, and its tight interior dimensions would be fine for people not known for their towering stature. The first 4CV rolled out of Hino's rudimentary factory on 28 March 1953, the first 100 cars being assembled from French-supplied kits. The seven-year contract allowed Hino to boost the 4CV's local content and, by 1957, when it was making over 3,500 a year, this reached 100 per cent.

The agreement, though, wasn't renewed. Renault always had a sniffy attitude towards Hino, which now decided to make a car of its own: the Contessa. The main component carried over was the 893cc 4CV engine, but to make the car a full five-seater and so attract more customers, the radiator was repositioned beyond the engine (instead of between the power unit and the rear bulkhead) in the Contessa's greatly elongated body. The 35bhp motor was tilted over to the left and used a crossflow head, while transmission was initially three-speed with a rather vague column-mounted shift, and later came a four-speeder.

Alongside the boxy saloon there was also the Hino 900 Sprint Coupé, with delightfully pretty Michelotti styling. It was equipped with a 45bhp engine worked over by Italian tuner Nardi and was said to be good for 87mph (the upright Contessa saloon did just 68 tops). It benefitted from a floor-mounted gear change. Although this Sprint was shown at motor shows worldwide, there were no sales outside Japan. Things were different for the replacement Contessa range of 1964, which was exported to right-hand drive (like Japan) markets in Australia and New Zealand. One of these found its way into the permanent collection of London's Science Museum. Hino, though, was taken over by Toyota in 1966, and the Contessa slowly phased out to make way for massive production of Toyota's Hi-Lux pick-up.

Above: The Scout introduced the novel concept of the sport-utility vehicle, or SUV.

Opposite: The Scout Traveltop was the first stage in converting the Scout pick-up into a leisure vehicle.

1961 INTERNATIONAL HARVESTER SCOUT 80

When International Harvester added a small pick-up to its truck range, nobody involved knew it would usher in a new genre of car: the sport-utility vehicle, or SUV. The Scout is indeed the grandaddy of them all. In retrospect, though, its genesis is a series of accidental stumbles.

A 1958 executive brainstorming session pinpointed a light, compact pick-up as a project with potentially 6,000–10,000 extra truck sales a year, partly inspired by the popularity of the civilian Jeep. The chassis engineering and two- and four-wheel drive drivetrain would be easy for the Fort Wayne, Indiana, company to handle, but there was no suitable engine, nor the tooling to make bodywork for this 'Small 4×4 Unit'. Initially, the thinking was to use a body moulded from Royalite plastic, and buy in the B Series engine from Austin in England. Indecision then swirled around the project until Ted Ornas, truck styling department head, produced some very attractive sketches, and momentum resurged. Rising confidence and sales forecasts meant IH felt it could afford to stamp the body panels from steel after all (quotes from plastics suppliers were too costly anyway). Meanwhile, an economical power unit was created by slicing the company's own V8 in half to make a slanted, 2.5-litre, four-cylinder. Axles, transfer case and three-speed manual gearbox were all bought in, and were similar to Jeep components.

Shortly before the Scout's launch on 21 November 1960 came concerns about cargo security. For urban duties, such as delivering liquor, a lifting tonneau cover was considered for the pick-up bed. Then a full-length hardtop was deemed more versatile, and this bolt-on 'Traveltop' was offered instead, forming a third variation to the range alongside an open-roofed roadster with folding windscreen, and a conventional 'half-cab' pick-up. Because there was a rigid bulkhead behind the seats, though, the Traveltop couldn't be considered a true station wagon despite its rear side windows.

The Scout was extremely basic, strictly an austere industrial working vehicle, and in this role it was in high demand. A heater and armrests were the only 'comfort' options, and they both cost extra. International Harvester was making 160 a day by March 1961, and there was a waiting list for the 4×4 Traveltop. The tops could also be retro-fitted to standard pick-ups.

Dealers were besieged with requests for a proper station wagon and this came, at first, as another kit for dealer retro-fitting, which involved removing the bulkhead, installing a rear bench seat, and fitting folding front bucket seats for rear access. Only for the 1963 model year was the complete package available ex-works, now also fitted with wind-up windows and called simply the International Scout. A soft-top convertible model was also added and, ta-da! Emerging just before the Jeep Wagoneer, the sport-utility vehicle was born.

Innovation is one thing, market dominance another. Although the Scout was made until 1980, it never achieved the success of Jeep or the 1964 Ford Bronco that it inspired. However, in an unexpected twist, Volkswagen has acquired the name and design rights, and a new Scout will soon be back on sale.

1961 CHRYSLER TURBOFLITE

This showpiece for the '61 New York Auto Show was also a vessel for Chrysler's early CR2A gas turbine engine, which led to the Chrysler Turbine (see p. 48). When the doors were opened, the entire cockpit roof, with its heat-reflecting glass, pivoted back towards the rear aerofoil to admit driver and passenger.

1961 ROVER T4

The fourth and last of Rover's gas turbine experimental cars was this four-door saloon. The 'jet' engine drove the front wheels and it was said to be capable of 140mph. It never went on sale, but the shape resurfaced two years later as the acclaimed Rover P6 2000 executive car.

Above: The front cover of the Talisman brochure stoked the keen driver image.

Opposite: The Talisman aimed to break free of the Tornado's kit car roots, and almost succeeded.

1961 TORNADO TALISMAN

Britain's cottage industry of kit car manufacturers, engine tuners and amateur racing drivers produced a few spectacular breakthroughs into the mainstream, particularly Colin Chapman's Lotus and the Cosworth high-performance engines of Mike Costin and Keith Duckworth. It all sprang from the country's ingenuity at an early form of recycling. Few 1950s enthusiasts could run to a brand-new sports car, but plenty could afford a rusty Ford Popular for £20, a plastic two-seater body for £60, and some chilly weekends in the garage to meld the two into a cut-price fun car. A clued-up spanner-man might then modify the engine for extra urge and in the 1950s, before the advent of the MoT, these home-made contraptions were often frighteningly fast – and sometimes even competitive in minor track events.

Taking a leaf out of Chapman's instruction manual, Bill Woodhouse and Tony Bullen sought to leave the kit car market behind with their Tornado Talisman. They'd started out in 1958 with the Tornado Typhoon body/chassis kit, which just needed the parts from a corrosion-riddled Ford 10 to come to life. These were better quality than many counterparts, and they sold 400 of them. The Talisman, though, launched in December 1961, was a gigantic step forward – a proper car whether supplied in kit form or fully factory finished.

Where the Typhoon looked homespun, the thoroughly engineered Talisman had an attractive, two-plus-two GT body that wouldn't have looked unbefitting outside any golf club. Woodhouse said later, in an interview in *Classic & Sportscar* magazine (February 1988): 'It was the nearest thing to the 1300cc Alfa Romeo Giulietta, except it out-performed the Alfa. Unfortunately, our extra 40cc meant we did not compete in the same class.' The interior was particularly neat, considering the resources available. Underpinning it was a ladder-type chassis supporting a tubular steel frame. All-round double wishbone independent suspension was specified, plus rack and pinion steering from the Triumph Herald, and front disc brakes. Cornering was impressive, the hard ride a little less so.

Under the bonnet was no less surprising; not the old Ford side-valve lump but an overhead-valve 1340cc Ford Consul Classic engine carefully developed by Cosworth (a standard one was offered too) with a unique camshaft and twin Weber carburettors. It's the first four-seater car ever fitted with a Cosworth power unit. About 75bhp was in prospect, with excellent mid-range torque, and many owners were eager to race these 90mph GTs in saloon events, winning respect if not many races outright in the motor sport community. However, a team of three did clinch the Six-Hour Relay race at Silverstone in 1962, a mighty achievement.

Things should have gone well, but Woodhouse later admitted the partners were too partial to going racing, and should have reinvested their profits in making the car itself, whose sound reputation gave it such good omens. By 1963 Woodhouse and Bullen opted for voluntary liquidation to get themselves out of financial ruin. They'd delivered 189 Talismans. It deserved much better: in kit form with Cosworth engine included, the car had cost £875, and just £1,259 ready-built when Lotus's own, somewhat fragile, Elite was £1,949. Car, company and founders are among the British motor industry's more tantalising might-have-beens …

Above: The Interlagos was Brazil's first sports car, and Emerson Fittipaldi honed his skills in one.

Opposite: The Alpine A108 convertible was also locally made by Willys Overland do Brasil.

1962 WILLYS INTERLAGOS

Knowledgeable classic car fans will no doubt do a double take at this one; has the author included photos of the highly coveted Alpine A108 in error? The cars do look similar and in fact are near identical because, without the Alpine, Brazil might never have got its very first sports car.

Alpine began life because of an ambitious young man called Jean Rédélé. The son of an important Renault dealer in Dieppe on France's Normandy coast, Jean already had his pilot's licence when he decided to tackle a few rallies in a Renault 4CV, starting in 1952. He was soon completely hooked, built his own, lighter two-door saloon, and proceeded to win his class with it on the 1954 Coupe Des Alpes rally. 'I had the most fun when I was winding through the Alps in my Renault 4CV,' he said. 'Consequently, I decided to call my future cars "Alpine". It had to be possible for my clients to discover this driving pleasure, at the wheel of the car I wanted to build.'

He launched his 4CV-based A106 a year later, farming out assembly and targeting motor sport-obsessed customers for his cars. Renault loved the halo effect they gave and was happy to support his independent enterprise, supplying all the mechanical parts young Jean needed for this elfin glass-fibre GT cars. He said, proudly: 'We proved that we could build them very light and very sturdy.'

The new A108 Berlinette came in 1958 with a lower, more aerodynamic body beautifully styled by Giovanni Michelotti, and the tuned 848cc engine from the Renault Dauphine Gordini. It had a fantastic power-to-weight ratio and was very nimble in expert hands, and so, despite the sub-1-litre engine capacity, it lapped up winding roads with gusto. Drivers enjoyed a snug and purposeful cockpit, the dashboard housing a tachometer, speedometer, fuel and temperature gauges.

Renault already had a deal with Willys Overland do Brasil to build the Dauphine under licence at its modern factory near Sao Paolo, and so it was straightforward to add the Alpine A108 to the South American line-up; the plastic body could easily be moulded locally and Willys – which, through close government connections and local shareholders, had a third of the local car market to itself – manufactured everything else.

The licence concession with Alpine began in 1962, and the partners decided to call the car the Interlagos after the local race circuit. Just as in France, there was a two-seater, a 2+2 and an open roadster version. This was the car the original generation of Brazilian racing drivers had at their disposal, most notably future Formula 1 great Emerson Fittipaldi. Willys built 822 examples of the Interlagos up to 1966, so it was never a common sight across such a vast country (the A108 was licence-built in Mexico, too). Back in France it had already been supplanted by the more powerful A110, which went on to enjoy a stellar career in world rallying, but that one never made it to Brazil, and shortly afterwards Renault cut its ties to the country after Willys changed hands in 1967 (see p. 131).

Above: The first BMW with the 'Hofmeister Kink', although that may also have been the 1500 …

Opposite: The only BMW 3200 CS convertible made, especially for BMW owner Herbert Quandt.

1962 BMW 3200 CS

One extremely important BMW made its debut at the 1961 Frankfurt motor show, a car that would be the foundation of all BMW's success to this present day. Officially the 1500, the company declared it the *Neue Klasse* (New Class), and that's exactly what it was: a compact, high-quality, fine-handling sports saloon for businessmen who felt themselves too youthful for a stuffy old Mercedes and yet too ambitious for an Opel Rekord.

In its shadow at Frankfurt, though, lurked another new Bee-Emm, a rarefied, hand-made machine with strong links back to the 1950s, when the Munich company almost went bust (only making motorbikes and the Isetta bubble car pulled it back from the brink). The 3200 CS didn't get much attention at the time, and it remains largely unacknowledged even now.

The legacy technology underpinning the 3200 CS was a traditional separate chassis frame, which dated back to the 501 luxury saloon of precisely ten years earlier, and the rest of the car was similar too, with its torsion bar suspension all-round, live rear axle, four-speed manual gearbox and a 3.2-litre V8 overhead-valve engine developing 160bhp.

Since 1956 there had been an imposing two-door, four-seater tourer in the BMW range called the 503, and the 3200 CS was its replacement. BMW's marketing manager Helmut Bonsch and chief engineer Fritz Fiedler decided the new car needed some styling panache, and that Italy was the place to get it. The *Neue Klasse* had been shaped by consultant Giovanni Michelotti, but for the 3200 CS they went to Bertone, who assigned a very young Giorgetto Giugiaro to style it and, considering the dimensional restrictions of the chassis frame itself, he did a wonderful job. You can see a lot of his later Alfa Romeo Giulia GT in the thin windscreen pillars and other details, as well as the overall form for subsequent BMW coupés over the next twenty-five years.

Bertone, moreover, had an even bigger role because the bodies were manufactured at its workshops in Turin, and shipped to BMW in Munich by rail for fitting to the chassis frames. Production began in January 1962 and lasted until September 1965, at which point 585 had been sold. Just one of these was a convertible, built especially as a gift for BMW majority shareholder Herbert Quandt. The *Neue Klasse* 2000 CS then replaced it with its fully integral construction and overhead-camshaft power unit; the 124mph 3200 CS was BMW's last pushrod-engined new car, and throughout its short life was barely promoted at all. It hardly ever appeared in a magazine road test, and there were no changes in its specification aside from a viscous clutch, wood-finished dashboard and leather upholstery after the first 175 cars built.

The 3200 CS and the *Neue Klasse* 1500 saloon did share one small detail that's been a famous BMW motif ever since. Near the base of the rearmost screen pillar was a distinctively shaped rearward/forward double angle to elegantly complete the rear side window aperture. Did it come from the pen of Giugiaro for the 3200 CS, or Michelotti for the 1500? They were revealed simultaneously, after all, so no wonder it's become known everywhere as the 'Hofmeister Kink', named after BMW's 1955–70 design manager Wilhelm Hofmeister, the secret ringmaster behind BMW's renaissance.

Above: The Deep Sanderson DS301, clearly showing where the whole rear body opened up.

Opposite: With its Mini engine and gearbox mid-mounted, the DS301 was a true ground-breaker.

1962 DEEP SANDERSON DS301

British engineer and racing driver Chris Lawrence had a career with its opening and closing highpoints both involving Morgan cars. Having gained his engineering degree in the Royal Navy, he spent every spare hour in the 1950s building and racing sports cars. After buying a second-hand Morgan Plus Four in 1958, his tuning modifications coaxed 50 per cent more power from its engine, and four years later he drove it to a faultless 2-litre class win at the Le Mans 24 Hours race, averaging 94mph.

Thirty-five years later, a still-grateful Morgan employed him to oversee its all-new Aero 8 sports car, and naturally his remit included taking it to Le Mans in 2002. He regarded the Aero 8 as the pinnacle of his career – more even than his 100 race wins and two Formula 1 starts – but had to retire early in 2003 and died of cancer eight years later.

In between, though, came the Deep Sanderson, and as such the first sports car to use the Mini's powerpack behind the driver, instead of up front.

Chris had already designed some Formula Junior racing cars, one with his patented 'Lawrence Link' rear suspension system. Switching focus to a road-going sports car, he used the Mini's front-wheel drive engine/transmission, perversely, at the back, for proven racecar-style weight distribution and roadholding, and his colleagues devised an equally unusual chassis, with a central 'backbone' tunnel, front and rear box sections, and an aluminium floor reinforced with steel tubes. A custom-made gear change gave it functionality, and the first prototype was an ugly open two-seater. Its extreme lightness meant a lowly 850cc engine, not even the Cooper one, was sufficient to give this road-legal go-kart 0–60mph acceleration in just nine seconds.

It took the 1962 Racing Car Show by storm, the way-out machine priced at just £951. One year later, the production version emerged, now a tiny fastback coupé, and the entire rear section of the body tipped open to access the engine.

A car was entered at Le Mans in 1963 but disqualified on somewhat nebulous grounds. Two Mini Cooper-powered 301s then contested Le Mans in 1964. One crashed out in practice sessions, and Chris and co-driver Gordon Spice lasted one hour in the other before blowing a head gasket. Not before it had hit 152mph on the Mulsanne Straight, mind.

There was genuine admiration for Chris's pioneering pluck, but the car was too ambitious and the budget too slim. For this truly was men-in-sheds stuff. He didn't have the space for an assembly line at his Acton, west London, premises so the cars, sold as kits, were assembled by his friend John Pearce in makeshift premises – and outdoors – in Southall, Middlesex. Only fifteen had been made when Lawrence suffered a serious crash on a French road, and his recovery meant he couldn't continue, although happily he later returned to his LawrenceTune engines business, and other projects. And why Deep Sanderson? It's a contraction of 'Deep Henderson' and Joan Sanderson – his father's favourite jazz track, and his mother's maiden name!

1962 FORD SEATTLE-ITE XXI

A six-wheeler that existed only as this five-eighths scale model, and was built specifically for Ford's display at the Seattle World's Fair. The futurist Alex Tremulis was its designer, and if the car had ever been made for real it was intended to have interchangeable power units – one electric and the other nuclear!

1962 FORD COUGAR

This gull-winged masterpiece, a working car with a 300bhp 6.6-litre V8 engine, was designed and built for Ford by leading Hollywood customiser Dean Jeffries. Retractable headlamps were another feature. Jeffries was to build a great many famous TV and film cars, including the Monkeemobile for pop group The Monkees.

Above: Ford's first front-drive car, from West Germany via Detroit.

Right: The Taunus 12m estate car; rear indicators flashed red, like many US cars.

1962 FORD TAUNUS P4 12M

For a pioneering car – the first Ford with front-wheel drive and a V4 engine – the Taunus 12M was treated with extraordinary indifference. Pushed from pillar to post within the sprawling multinational, its undoubted merits seemed to please no one.

These were chaotic times in a Detroit anxious for smaller, more fuel-efficient cars with, at that time, appeal to women drivers and the swelling number of converts to the imported Volkswagen Beetle. Working against this was the sound logic that small, economical cars generated slim profits, and left car salesmen sour and unmotivated.

Ford, though, got down to earnest business with its P4 'Cardinal' project in 1959 to combat the Beetle head on; a 'sub-compact' to the upcoming Ford Falcon 'compact'. It immediately decided, surely influenced by the Mini, that a space-efficient, front-wheel drivetrain would give a roomy small car with stable handling. The engine was to be a 1.2-litre, four-cylinder, positioned ahead of the front axle line, and with a 60-degree V-formation to make it as small as possible. The front suspension arms, unusually, were connected to the engine block, and then also to a crossmember linked to the floorpan.

The car, as a two-door saloon, got the go-ahead in 1960, with plans to build it in the Kentucky plant that previously hosted the ill-fated Edsel. Simultaneously, at Ford of Germany, plans were afoot for its own, all-new small car to take on the Beetle and impending Opel Kadett A on its home turf. These were suddenly skewered by US HQ and the Germans were obliged to adopt a version of the Cardinal, as well as share the final development, handle the styling, and manufacture parts for both. The Cardinal was almost the same size as their very successful rear-wheel drive Taunus 17M, and not at all the small car the unhappy Germans wanted, but they were forced to accept it.

Then the bombshell. Incoming Ford top brass didn't like the Cardinal (nor the Falcon), and all efforts were centred on what became the Ford Mustang. There would now be no US-built Cardinal and the car was launched as the German-built Taunus 12M. It wasn't even exported to North America! At first it was made in Cologne, but manufacture was soon pushed out to Ford's new factory in Genk, Belgium.

Announced on 15 September 1962, the 12M had a mixed reception. It was quite heavy and sluggish, with an unrefined and noisy engine, but its ride was soft and it was spacious inside. Top speed was 78mph. Although the handling was ultimately very safe, the nose-heavy 12M tended to pitch into corners, and customer alarm over this triggered a major suspension rethink. This was also to counter vibrations arising from rough road surfaces and felt via the steering. The ride/handling never seemed quite right. Then again, these were early steps for the European front-drive breed; it took many years for makers like Fiat and Renault to perfect the set-up.

Jarring (to Europe) Americanisms were the front bench seat, column gear change, strip speedo, dished steering wheel and rear lights where the red bulb flashed as an indicator. A four-door saloon, fastback coupé, two-door estate and a van were added, plus a 1.5-litre engine, and front disc brakes appeared in 1964. Sales over four years exceeded 680,000, respectable but chickenfeed besides the millions of Beetles being shifted. Heavily reworked as the P6 12M Taunus, it limped on until 1970, and front-wheel drive wasn't revisited until the 1976 Fiesta.

Above: The engine is in the back of the Colt 600 as Mitsubishi's family car grows up.

Opposite: The Mitsubishi Colt 600 strutting its stuff in the 1963 Malaysian Grand Prix.

1962 MITSUBISHI COLT 600

Mitsubishi claims to be Japan's first serious manufacturer of motor cars. OK, it may have simply copied the Fiat Tipo 3 for its Model A of 1917, and hand built just twenty-two of them until 1921, but it still counts. Its first motor car for customers of the modern era arrived in 1960. The 500 was an austere four-seater economy machine with an air-cooled, 493cc two-cylinder in its rounded rump, driving the rear wheels and trailing a haze of blue smoke that betrayed its two-stroke movement. Monocoque construction made it light yet strong, and the three-speed gearbox could row it along to a top speed of 62mph.

A 500 Super Deluxe came with a throatier, 594cc motor and swifter acceleration, and it made news when the type took the top four places in the sub-750cc class of the 1962 Macao Grand Prix.

The 500 faced a tricky issue, though. It had been conceived in answer to a government call for a 'national vehicle', and created from scratch by a team of mostly ex-aircraft engineers, working in a dusty attic at the Shin Mitsubishi Heavy Industries head office in Nagoya. The 500 was the first Japanese car to undergo wind tunnel tests to check its aerodynamics, but the designers made a strategic mistake by increasing the proposed engine size after being impressed by the 1957 Fiat Nuova 500. This made it too powerful for the tax-friendly *Kei* category of city cars, shutting it out of the most popular stratum of the new car market. Poor sales forced Mitsubishi into an emergency rethink and in 1962 it produced two new small cars: the extremely tiny Minica that really was a *Kei* car, and a thoroughly revamped 500 Super Deluxe called the Colt 600. The Colt sub-brand was used on many subsequent Mitsubishis, and was even used in place of Mitsubishi for ten years of UK sales. Here, though, is where it started …

Alluding to a frisky young horse seemed ambitious, but once again Mitsubishi gamely took to Far Eastern circuits and found success; the Colt 600 finished second and third in the 1963 Malaysian Grand Prix, and scored a victory the year after in the under-600cc class.

With its two-door bodywork extended and enlarged front and back, the Colt 600 aimed for design convention as a small family saloon. There was a front bench seat and steering column gear shift so it could squash in five (of average Japanese height) people, plus a bigger fuel tank. The overhead-valve engine, though, was unaltered, still found at the back, while top whack remained 62mph. Upon its debut at the 1962 Tokyo motor show, Mitsubishi exhibited a Colt 600 convertible, but it was destined never to actually go on sale; the company built a faithful replica of it in 2005.

The Colt 600 proved an uncomfortable stopgap until a new fastback Colt 800 came along in 1965, although even that car stuck to a two-stroke engine, albeit now water-cooled, for a few more years yet as Mitsubishi edged cautiously into the motoring mainstream.

Above: The Sabre Six as announced, although the majority would be fixed-roof coupés.

Opposite: The original Sabre featured these fang-like front overriders and a 1.7-litre Consul engine.

1962 RELIANT SABRE SIX

Here's a powerful and characterful sports car that typifies the ingenious approach of Britain's many small-scale companies of the 1960s. It's an ancestor of the Reliant Scimitar GT and Scimitar GTE, the latter being the ground-breaking sports estate beloved of Princess Anne, the Princess Royal. The Sabre has a fascinating tale to tell that stretches from Staffordshire to Haifa in Israel and Beverly Hills in LA.

It owes its existence to one Yitzhak Shubinsky, founder of Autocars Ltd, still the only significant car company ever to be Israeli-based. With all the independent fervour surrounding his country's establishment, Shubinsky opened a factory to make small utility vehicles, including a van, station wagon and pick-up all designed by Reliant in Tamworth, and through patriotism many Tel Aviv organisations felt compelled to buy them.

Shubinsky wanted more. While visiting the Racing Car Show in London in 1960, he took keen note of the stylish Ashley 1172 kit car body and also a new ladder-frame chassis with a clever independent front suspension schemed by engineer Leslie Ballamy. His brainwave was to bring the two together to make a two-seater sports car he could build in Haifa and export to the States. Reliant was roped in again, and suggested a 1.7-litre four-cylinder engine from the Ford Consul paired with a ZF four-speed gearbox, all-synchromesh and German made. Agreements were reached with Ashley Laminates and Mr Ballamy, and a prototype was running only nine months later. For something so cobbled together, it came out remarkably well, although the fang-like overriders on the car's nose exuded a bizarre appearance.

Autocars' sports car had its maiden appearance during the World's Trade Fair held at New York's Coliseum in May 1961, and it was called the Sabra after a cactus native to Israel. Reliant built the first 100 cars, and shipped them off to Sabra Motors in California; then it transferred production by sending complete kits for assembly in Haifa.

Reliant itself marketed the car at home, launching its Sabre 4 at the 1961 London Motor Show. An optional twin-carburettor engine upgrade turned it into a 100mph car and spurred on Reliant to enter some rallies, including the 1962 Tulip and RAC, and the 1963 Monte Carlo. A coupé version and a less disturbing nose design were added. It was fun but expensive at £1,128, and didn't sell well. In three years just 208, overwhelmingly GTs, found buyers. It actually bombed in the US too, with just forty-one more Israeli-built Sabras shipped there.

So the Sabre Six was a last chance try. Using the coupé body (just two were open roadsters) with short-nose bonnet and round wheelarches, the engine was the 2.6-litre straight-six from the Ford Zephyr MkIII and that car's four-speed-plus-overdrive gearbox, with a replacement Triumph TR4-shared front suspension after the first fifteen cars. It was good for 110mph, and won widespread praise. The kit car roots remained, though, and just seventy-seven were sold before Reliant moved on to its more credible Scimitars. The last Israeli Sabra was built in 1968, by the way, and Shubinsky's company folded three years later.

Above: The Winchester was tall enough to accommodate most hats; two-tone paint a natty option.

Opposite: This shiny new Winchester is being crated up for export to the USA.

1962 WINCHESTER TAXI

This vehicle was created by an insurance company to settle a grudge. Few people outside the London taxi trade have ever driven one, and even the paying passengers didn't notice it much as they were carried home drunk from Park Lane to the suburbs. It managed to be crude and innovative at the same time.

The Owner Drivers' Society was a trade body for cabbies who bought their own taxicabs, rather than working for a fleet, and in 1960 they were getting frustrated. The Austin FX4 introduced two years before enjoyed a market monopoly, and was judged rust prone, unreliable and expensive to fix. Cab drivers were practically held to ransom when it came to outgoings and purchase price for the 600 taxis ordered annually to replace any that were ten years old, and therefore ending their roadworthy lives. The Public Carriage Office insisted on vehicles with a 25ft turning circle, five passenger seats and headroom lofty enough to take top-hatted men to Claridge's or the Reform Club; no ordinary car or van could be used instead.

Refusing any longer to be a captive market, the Society's in-house Westminster Insurance company decided to commission a new vehicle for its members. A key aspect was it should have a glass fibre bodyshell, to vastly cut the costs of inevitable accident repairs and replacement steel panels. It chose James Whitson & Co. of West Drayton near Heathrow Airport as the contractor. Whitson was experienced in making glass-reinforced shells for sports cars, buses and lorries, and manufactured bodies for the standby 'Green Goddess' fire engines.

Working to Westminster's outline, Whitson built the first taxi body from aluminium sheet, from which it then took the glass fibre moulds. The design wouldn't win any beauty contests, and surprisingly the driving position was cramped and uncomfortable. The floor and window frames were wooden. The old-fashioned separate chassis featured robust leaf springs and a rattly Perkins 4/99 diesel engine. The insurance firm couldn't use the Westminster name, as Austin already had rights to that, so they called its offshoot Winchester Automobiles (West End) Ltd, and from 1962 it operated from premises in Lots Road, Chelsea. Each basic cab was taken there to be completed. It was a shambolic business: lights and switches were bought from local motor factors' shops, and almost no two Winchesters were alike. Build quality was by all accounts appalling.

The amateurish operation shifted into MkII mode in 1965 after sixty-five cabs had been delivered, but only with the MkIII did the Winchester's lame on-road performance improve thanks to a new chassis with the Ford Transit's 1.7-litre V4 engine and four-speed gearbox.

The Winchester proves you shouldn't take moaning London taxi drivers seriously. They said they wanted their own cab but, when they got one, flawed though it was, they shunned it. In two years, for example, only a dozen new MkIIIs joined the capital's ranks. Curiously, Winchesters often pop up in old British films and TV series. That's because diesel engines used to interfere badly with sound-recording equipment, and the Winchester MkIII was the only taxi with a relatively quiet petrol engine …

1963 FORD ALLEGRO

Ten years before Austin used the Allegro name came this Italian-looking but US-designed coupé. It used the V4 engine and front-wheel drive from the Ford Taunus 12M (see p. 38), whose abandoned US launch it should have supported. Inside, the seats were fixed, with the steering wheel and pedals adjustable to fit any driver.

1963 JAGUAR E-TYPE LIGHTWEIGHT

An E-type with a dramatic twist: of just twelve Lightweight cars built for racing, this unique example had a low-drag body designed by Jaguar's aerodynamics genius Malcolm Sayer. Built for German driver Peter Lindner, it failed in his bid for glory in the 1964 Le Mans 24 Hours, despite having the most powerful XK engine, at 344bhp, that Jaguar ever made.

Above: The Turbines covered 1.1 million road miles in the hands of 203 'ordinary' drivers.

Right: All fifty-five cars had Ghia-built bodies, painted Turbine bronze.

1963 CHRYSLER TURBINE

Chrysler's Turbine project remains the boldest, most glamorous rolling experiment ever conducted on American roads. The only car ever series-produced with a gas turbine 'jet' engine, the real-life test programme went as smoothly as the power delivery from its vibration-free power unit.

Selling this exceptional machine to the general public was deemed too risky, so instead Chrysler loaned examples out for free, for three-month trial periods, to a wide spectrum of American drivers; accountants Touche Ross vetted them for trustworthiness, and the first was delivered to Richard Vlaha in Broadview, Illinois, on 29 October 1963. In the end the cars were used in 133 cities across forty-eight states. The 'pre-flight' training given was quite extensive, because there was an eight-step starting procedure just to get the car running.

Rather than install the US corporation's fourth-generation (there were seven in total) turbine engines in a standard Chrysler, a unique model was designed in-house. Then fifty-five bodies were built by Italian coachbuilder Ghia and shipped to Detroit, where the powerpacks were fitted at the front, driving the rear wheels. The Turbine was a restrained-looking four-seater hardtop with, ironically, little of the jet-age gimmickry usually adorning Chrysler/Ghia show cars. They were all painted in an identical colour named 'Turbine Bronze' with matching interiors.

Engine turbine rotation of up to 45,700rpm was reined back, using a gear-reduction unit, to a maximum in daily driving use of 4,680rpm, delivered via a lightly modified automatic gearbox. The 130bhp engine could burn any fuel, including diesel, alcohol, perfume, peanut oil or vegetable fat, although usually regular JP-4 aircraft kerosene was used.

The test cars covered 1.1 million miles with 203 different drivers including twenty women. They proved remarkably reliable, with only 5 per cent of the total test time lost to breakdowns, and oil changes completely unnecessary.

'With no carburettor, you don't pump the throttle as you would for other cars of the era,' reported Todd Lassa of *Motor Trend* magazine. 'Acceleration is progressive and oh-so-smooth, but it's not terribly quick. Drivers will marvel at the sound rather than the forward thrust.'

There were a few downsides, however, which included patchy running at high altitudes and the vacuum cleaner-like noise. But the biggest problem was the unacceptably high level of nitrogen oxide emissions.

After the programme ended in September 1966, forty-six Turbines were scrapped. Chrysler didn't want its research vehicles ending up on second-hand car lots. Today, three working cars survive in the company's own collection. Four more went to museums, including the Detroit Historical, Smithsonian Institute, St Louis Museum of Transportation and the Peterson Museum, while two are treasured privately, one in the Blackhawk Collection and the other by celebrity collector Jay Leno. Of these, four are also still fully functioning.

Chrysler did build further turbine-engined prototypes, even fixing the emissions problems, but its financial troubles meant the Turbine adventure was never repeated. The enormous cost of materials and castings for making the motors over conventional internal combustion engines ensured that no turbine-engined car has ever been available from a showroom, and is never likely to be.

Below: A rare two-door Corsair with model Jean Shrimpton and F1 champion Jim Clark.

Opposite: The attractive Corsair convertible was by Crayford of Westerham, Kent.

1963 FORD CONSUL CORSAIR

Corsairs have vanished, decimated by tinny construction, rampant rust and indifference, but memories of this strikingly styled car remain vivid, And not just because it's the one the infamous Lord Lucan used to make his getaway to the coast (we believe …) and his own disappearance. So why is it in this book?

The answer lies in this two-door version, seldom seen when new and today a classic car unicorn. The Corsair was unveiled at the London Motor Show in 1963 in both two- and four-door formats, yet the former was an oddity. If you wanted one, your Ford dealer had to specially notify the factory in Halewood on Merseyside to make it for you, whether in standard (only 335 made!), Deluxe or GT guise. They weren't built to sit around in showrooms, where they'd be unlikely to shift.

Most two-doors were for export to Scandinavia, where a two-door Corsair S mixed Deluxe trim with a 1500GT engine. Across northern Europe, well-specified two-door saloons sold strongly, from Volvos to Opels, and especially the German-built Ford Taunus 17M. Britain's Corsair tried to join that group, but never did catch on abroad.

It was introduced as a bridgehead between the Cortina and Zephyr 4 in Ford's range, replacing the Consul Classic and being, according to Ford chairman Sir Terence Beckett: 'An extension of the Cortina formula.' Indeed, the Corsair (code name Project Buccaneer) relied on a Cortina MkI floorpan and inner structure, to include door frames and side glass in a longer body, with wedge nose, truncated tail and sunken headlights evoking the opulent Ford Thunderbird from the other side of the Atlantic. The vertical tail lights and arrow-like side profile seemed modern and upmarket, quite unlike the cheaper Cortina. Formula 1 World Champion Jim Clark toasted the first one off the line with champagne in October 1963.

The 1.5-litre engine came from the Ford Cortina Super too, with 60bhp in standard form and 78bhp as a GT with twin-choke Weber carburettor. This GT was a vivacious, enjoyable car, capable of 95mph and with a floor-mounted gear change as standard (others came with an undesirable column shift), plus an inconveniently positioned rev counter; they all had front disc brakes.

By the time the Corsair V4 came along in 1965, the two-doors had gone, as had the Consul part of its title. The 1.7- and 2.0-litre cars were more lively, but these V4 engines, shared with the Transit van, were rather unrefined. The Corsair lasted until 1970, and with 330,735 examples made – two-doors accounted for one in every seven cars – it was still regarded as a decent motor right up to its demise. Its place in Ford's line-up was then largely taken by the Capri.

The two-door was ideal for conversion into a five-seater convertible; done not by Ford itself but specialist coachbuilder Crayford of Westerham, Kent. It looked graceful with the hood folded out of sight, and the work was well executed, beefed up internally to compensate for any loss of strength after cutting the roof off (doing that to a four-door saloon is impossibly difficult). Some 200 of these open-air beauties were sold.

Below: The IM3 was one of several British cars built for the Italian market by Innocenti of Milan.

Opposite: Subtle changes to bumpers, grille, headlights and side trim set the IM3 apart.

1963 INNOCENTI MORRIS IM3

For the third time, the Milan home of Lambretta scooters had taken an already acclaimed British car and added some clever dashes of Italian pizzazz to it. Because the closer you looked at the IM3 compared to a British Morris 1100, the more desirable it started to appear.

First there were the stacked headlight/sidelight units either side of a redesigned, wider radiator grille, which imparted a bit of Mercedes-Benz-like prestige. Then there were slimline, wraparound bumpers with overriders and chrome body-side strips that craftily lifted the otherwise rather dumpy look. Inside, the plump and contoured seats and all-over carpeting were much more inviting, while the satin-finish instrument binnacle and three-spoke, drilled steering wheel exuded a sporty air.

And that steering wheel? Unlike in the Morris 1100, where it gave the feeling of driving a milk float, the wheel was upright and purposeful, thanks to a redesigned column with a universal joint to get the angle right. Pop the bonnet and there was an MG 1100-spec twin-SU HS2 carburettor engine, with a peppy 55bhp to bring alive the sure-footed, front-wheel drive handling.

Not that anyone back in the UK would have known about the Morris IM3; it was strictly for the Italian market. Beginning with the Austin A40, Innocenti first signed an agreement to make British Motor Corporation cars under licence in 1960. It was assembled alongside Lambretta scooters, and Innocenti soon spotted a great way to improve the car by adding a top-hinged tailgate at the back to make it one of the very first 'hatchbacks'. Next, in 1961, it added the Austin-Healey Sprite to its roster, and for this commissioned a brand-new body to make its own Innocenti 950 Spider. The IM3, denoted by its name and introduced in April 1963, then became the third British adaptation.

Although a very plain exact counterpart to the no-nonsense British Austin 1100, the Innocenti I4, joined the range in November 1964, the Italians always tried to keep their Morris IM3 aloft of the peasant herd. In 1965, for example, the option of Italian-made Dell'Orto FZD twin carburettors was introduced, and then in August 1966 the car was upgraded to be the IM3S, losing the overriders but gaining a restyled grille.

This car was an interesting success in a country where almost everyone drove a Fiat of some kind. Despite costing more than a higher powered Fiat 1500 saloon, the Morris IM3 had the considerable novelty of being front-driven with a transverse engine, and Fiat offered nothing as hi-tech until the 128 of 1968. Meanwhile, for buyers who valued a compact urban car where style, finish and exclusivity mattered more than higher speed, the IM3 was uniquely attractive.

It was available until 1970 and was among the final tally of 65,808 Italian-made editions of the BMC 1100 design. Long before that, though, Innocenti had started manufacturing Minis and, after its experience jazzing up the Morris 1100, those it built in Turin were generally of smarter detail design, and even better quality, than the British originals.

Below: Hidden under the floor of the Spider was the first rotary engine in any production car.

Opposite: Red or white were the only two colours available for NSU's hi-tech gamechanger.

1963 NSU WANKEL SPIDER

A rotary is an engine of supreme mechanical elegance, and its exceptional refinement is down, in part, to using a quarter of the moving parts of a conventional piston engine; there are, for example, no valves or crankshaft. It was invented by Dr Felix Wankel, and this is the world's first production car fitted with one.

Wankel's rotary engine employed a single, shallow combustion chamber housing – oval-shaped with pinched-in sides – in which a near-triangular rotor spun eccentrically. The tips of the rotor touched the sides of the chamber constantly as it span, the combustion cycle taking place in the ever-expanding and contracting cavities between them; ports in the chamber wall gave induction and exhaust like a two-stroke engine. The capacity on this NSU's engine was given as 497cc; equivalent to about 1000cc in any other car.

Each revolution of the triangular rotor caused three combustions and, because the output shaft was geared to revolve three times for each revolution of the rotor, one combustion stroke was produced for each revolution. Hence the power delivery was very smooth.

Dr Wankel was a largely self-taught workaholic who conceived all this in the 1920s, building his first working specimen in 1934. NSU of Neckarsulm, West Germany, was first drawn to his findings as a way to boost performance of its racing motorbikes; he then joined forces with NSU's Walter Froede, a prototype engine was running on a testbench by 1957, and the partners resolved to fix all the teething troubles together. Two years later, an anonymous, green NSU Prinz car equipped with a rotary engine embarked on the first real-world road tests.

By putting the engine into small-scale production in a specialist sports car, however, Froede sensibly felt its reliability could be assessed without jeopardising NSU's profitable manufacturing business.

The Spider hit the headlines in September 1963 at the Frankfurt motor show, production starting the following year. Derived from the existing, Bertone-styled Sport Prinz coupé, only the open Spider was rotary-powered. The tiny Wankel engine was mounted under the boot floor at the back: the 125kg (275lb) powertrain was so compact there was boot space at both front and rear.

On 50bhp the Spider could almost reach 100mph. What it lacked in torque it made up for in free-revving smoothness, spinning happily to 8,000rpm. In effect, it had the urge and refinement of a six-cylinder luxury car. Critics praised its power delivery and handling, but the Spider, like all early rotaries, was abnormally thirsty. Felix Wankel, though, never experienced driving it on open roads; his boffin focus was on research, science and patents, and he never even had a driving licence.

The rotary's downsides were its high petrol and oil consumption, premature damage to the rotor tips, and heavy emissions, although much of this was fixed subsequently. After a mere 2,375 Spiders had been sold – because even with some motor sport success, and a choice of red or white paintwork, paying customers remained wary – NSU moved on to its twin-rotor-engined Ro80 in 1967. The Spider was a genuine watershed in motoring history, yet it paid a steep penalty for breaking new ground.

1963 CHEVROLET CORVAIR MONZA GT

Sharing exactly the same tilt-forward windscreen/roof feature as the Testudo opposite, General Motors' own Corvair (see p. 78) two-seater was said to be a 149mph car. Two examples were made, the other one a red roadster, and together they conducted the circuit-opening ceremony at the 1963 Elkhart Lake 500 Race.

1963 BERTONE CHEVROLET CORVAIR TESTUDO

The magic feature of Bertone's show car was its cockpit access, which was gained by doors, roof and windscreen all tilting forward in one complete section. It also had pop-up headlights. It was fully working, too, and made its debut at the 1963 Geneva motor show after first being driven there over the Alps from Turin.

Below: Outdoor larks with Studebaker; a step leads on to an open-topped luggage area.

Opposite: The Lark Wagonaire was one of the last new Studebakers before its 1966 closure.

1963 STUDEBAKER LARK WAGONAIRE

If you'd ever needed to carry something extra tall in your estate car, then the Wagonaire would have been perfect. Just picture the typical American refrigerator, or a potted palm tree; even the largest station wagons would struggle.

The Wagonaire coped thanks to its sliding retractable roof panel over the cargo area, meaning the only height restriction would have been freeway bridges.

The idea came not from within the old-established Studebaker itself but the lively mind of industrial design consultant Brooks Stevens. In 1959 Stevens had been commissioned by the Olin Mathieson conglomerate to produce three show cars, intended to give automotive industry customers inspiration for using more aluminium components. These three Scimitar vehicles included an 'All-Purpose Sedan' with a sliding rear roof section. Studebaker was one of his other clients and, when it asked Stevens for some low-cost hacks to boost its flagging fortunes, he recycled the idea for the Studebaker Lark. It certainly was a feature no competitor could match, and the Wagonaire was an addition to the 1963 Lark range.

A neat folding step was incorporated into the tailgate's interior panel to give easy access to the cargo bed, and the roof panel slid forward manually before locking into position above the rear passenger seat, to leave the rear of the car completely open-topped. It was available in Standard, Regal or Daytona trim levels for 1963, evolving into the Challenger, Commander and Daytona for 1964, and it was a full six-seater (or five with optional front bucket seats). Engine choices were a 2.8-litre straight-six and 4.2- and 4.7-litre V8s, and if you opted for the big supercharged V8 then the extra-cost front disc brakes were advisable.

For its first year, the Wagonaire saw strong sales with over 11,000 delivered, as customers were drawn into showrooms to try out the novelty. This included a fleet of thirty sold to Movietone News for use as versatile mobile camera cars. Events, however, quickly conspired against the Wagonaire. The most seismic was Studebaker's decision to shut its South Bend, Indiana, factory in spring 1964 and relocate all remaining car production – Wagonaire included – to Ontario in Canada. This saw 1964-model sales halve to 5,163.

To compound the malaise, the word was out among potential customers that the water seeping in through the leading edge of the roof panel was down to drainage channels blocking up easily with nature's debris – almost certainly due to the rushed, low-budget design. Dealers did remind owners to maintain them properly, but the caveat was generally not happily received! This forced Studebaker to offer a welded up, fixed-roof alternative as a Wagonaire 'delete option'; all a bit embarrassing, and only 1,824 1965 models were sold, a handful with a rear-facing extra bench seat right at the back to make them seven/eight-seaters for huge families. Finally, the firm decided to halt all car making in March 1966 after just 940 more Wagonaires had been delivered.

An interesting but noble failure, then; or perhaps a car for practical uses that, in reality, were so infrequent potential buyers rightly decided they didn't really need a Wagonaire.

Above: Gondola but not forgotten? The Venezia makes its unusual debut.

Opposite: Shades of Lancia in this view of the Venezia prototype, photographed in the UK.

1963 SUNBEAM VENEZIA

On 9 September 1963 the Sunbeam Venezia made motoring history in an extraordinary way. It became the first car ever to grace the geometric stone paving of Piazza San Marco in Venice, having travelled there by gondola. The city's mayor and the British ambassador were in attendance to see this Anglo-Italian GT disembark to take its elegant bow. As were many pigeons. Plus another Brit, with the highly unfitting name of George Carless.

This pretty four-seater coupé was Carless's baby, on which he pinned high hopes for British fortunes in Italy. He ran the Italian import division of Britain's Rootes Group in 1960–65 and, because of steep import tariffs between the two countries, that was a tough task. However, a way around trade restrictions was found: starting in 1961, up to ten Hillman Super Minx saloons and four Sunbeam Alpine sports cars were assembled daily in the Nova Milanese factory of coachbuilder Carrozzeria Touring – already famous in England for the Aston Martin DB4 styling – alongside several desirable Alfa Romeos and Lancias.

Touring stamped the metal panels and most other parts were shipped over from Coventry to meet local-content quotas, giving Carless a Super Minx to market at a competitive price. He immediately sold 100 of them, painted green and black, into Milan's taxi trade. For the Italian-made Alpine, meanwhile, Touring instigated some excellent improvements, redesigning the tail end of the car to eradicate its dated-looking tailfins, enlarging boot and fuel tank capacity, and fitting a wooden dashboard and wood-rimmed steering wheel. Indeed, all the Touring redesign work would reappear in the British Alpine Series IV in 1964.

Being party to all this activity gave Carless an idea: why not get Touring to fit one of its stylish bodies on to a Rootes car, to make a sports saloon exclusive to Italy? Touring's designers Frederico Formenti and Aquilino Gilardi produced a 1:10 scale model looking like a smaller Lancia Flaminia, and in late 1961 it won approval back home from Lord Rootes. With British engineer Alec Caine as go-between, a Touring prototype was in Coventry by mid-1962, and after various detail modifications it was ready to be produced as a limited edition of 300 cars.

The Venezia's aluminium body was built around a tubular *superleggera* (super-light) frame riding on the floorpan of the Humber Sceptre, essentially a Super Minx with an 88bhp 1.6-litre engine. Windscreen, headlights and grille were identifiably from the Sceptre, but everything else oozed classic Italian GT. A racing car-like oil cooler was fitted, although hardly necessary, and there was overdrive as standard, yet no synchromesh on first gear.

Of course, because of those trade barriers, it was unfeasible to import the Venezia to the UK. And anyway, the Venezia was expensive for its modest performance, costing more than a Jaguar Mk2 2.4-litre. But strikes and cashflow issues at Rootes, and then at Touring, really hastened its demise, with 145 Sceptre-based cars made and fifty more using the less powerful Super Minx chassis. Rootes was taken over by Chrysler and Carrozzeria Touring went bankrupt by 1966. The cars are collectable today; cheap to restore for their Rootes mechanical parts but expensive to rectify that time-ravaged *superleggera* coachwork.

Above: Enlightened view: the five-door Primula was Fiat's front-wheel drive testbed.

Opposite: This Primula Coupé had the full coach-built treatment and a 75bhp 1.5-litre engine.

1964 AUTOBIANCHI PRIMULA

If proof was ever needed of the game-changing influence of the BMC Mini then the Primula was the first piece of substantial evidence. All previous Fiats had been rear-wheel drive cars with in-line engines at the front (larger cars) or back (smaller ones). The Primula, though, keenly adopted the Mini's front-wheel drivetrain with a transversely mounted engine. And it then defined the template for the typical family car that prevailed for the next forty years.

Autobianchi was founded in 1955 at Desio, Turin, a three-way joint venture between former bicycle makers the Bianchi family, tyres giant Pirelli, and Fiat. The intention, at first, was to make a jazzed up version of the Fiat 500 called the Bianchina. That suited all the stakeholders fine, and the cars were popular, but, for Fiat, Autobianchi represented a sensible place to test out new ideas, and among the first was plastic body panels. And it was the spectacular success of the Mini and BMC 1100 that made Fiat think Autobianchi made a good testbed for something similar in the Primula.

Fiat chief designer Dante Giacosa oversaw it, and the only difference he insisted on – to improve transmission noise and raise refinement – was to move the gearbox from under the engine in its oil sump, as for the Mini, and place it end-on to the Fiat 1.2-litre four-cylinder engine. This he achieved with unequal-length driveshafts to each front wheel, and a compact clutch. Everyone who drove one was mightily impressed with its sharp and sure-footed characteristics.

The company's product planners then scored a blinder by supplementing two- and four-door saloons with visually identical cars boasting a top-hinged tailgate. These roomy hatchbacks became Europe's first in the 'supermini' idiom typified by the Ford Fiesta that would shortly dominate the market. What's more, unlike many others to come, the Primula's hatchbacks opened down to floor level – no huffing and puffing needed to hoick luggage over a high sill.

In six years on sale, the Primula range enjoyed steady popularity, selling some 75,000 examples. In 1965 it came second in the European Car of the Year contest, behind the new BMC 1800, which must have felt disappointing. For Fiat, though, it was an excellent way to be satisfied with proof of concept and iron out any teething troubles without risking the reputation of its big-selling conventional cars like the 124. Once completely happy that the Primula worked a treat, the format was launched on the mainstream Fiat 128 in 1969.

All Primulas had four-wheel disc brakes and a sealed cooling system. The car greased itself automatically, too, which in those days was still a major boon maintenance-wise. Autobianchi added a sporty model to the range in 1965. The two-door coupé was beautifully built in Milan by Carrozzeria Touring and, besides its 1.5-litre engine with a peppy 75bhp (always overhead-valve rather than overhead-camshaft as in most other performance Fiats), came with a gleaming coachbuilder's paintjob and chrome wire wheels. In two years just 2,000 of these were made; like all Primulas, it was a notorious rust bucket, which is why you almost never come across any survivors.

Above: New bodywork front and back was intended to disguise the Torino's Anglia roots.

Opposite: Worth a second look? Torino was also a clever way to beat import tariffs.

1964 FORD ANGLIA TORINO

American super-salesman Filmer Melbourne Paradise certainly came up with the goods for Ford, his employer. Boasting a first-class economics degree, he was dispatched to Italy in 1953 to rev up Ford's business there, and with imported German- and British-made cars clawed his way to a 5 per cent market share – no mean feat when the European Common Market (which didn't include the UK) was in its infancy, and Fiat dominated Italy's roads.

The British-built Anglia 105E, in particular, proved popular for Ford Italiana, and in 1960 and '61 it was Italy's number one imported car. Just as quickly, its fortunes plummeted, and Paradise deduced this the fault of its styling, with its tailfins, reverse-rake rear window and fish-like frontage. After three years he maintained it was dating inexorably, and he had a rescue plan that involved making a new version exclusively for style-conscious Italians.

Rather surprisingly, Ford approved his scheme, and Paradise appointed renowned freelance designer Giovanni Michelotti to reimagine the Anglia. With plain and boxy lines front and back, Michelotti eliminated the Anglia's stylistic quirks and chrome-plated accents, most notably its eye-catching pointed back window. Externally, only the doors and windscreen were carried over, although structurally the car was unaltered, and so still narrow by prevailing standards. New circular rear light clusters resembled those on contemporary Ferraris. Nowadays the effect, next to the original, is pretty bland, but at the time it was thought to be a massive European improvement on the Americanised original.

Paradise called it the Anglia Torino, signifying the new version would be assembled at the Officine Stampaggi Industriali (OSI) plant in Turin, controlled jointly by Ghia and Olivetti. By bringing over only mechanical components from the UK, and using Italian labour, import duties were lowered to make the car even more competitive. There were two versions, the standard one with the responsive 997cc 'Kent' engine, and a more feisty Torino S with a twin-choke downdraught Weber carburettor and four-branch exhaust manifold. Both came with the equally good manual gearbox – the first in any affordable British small car with synchromesh on all four gears. In fact, this superb engine/gearbox combination played a big part in Britain's flourishing motor sport industry in the early 1960s, in Formula Ford and Formula Junior, and in powering Lotus cars and forming the basis of the first Cosworth engines.

Sales started strongly in 1965, with 2,847 Torinos delivered, and swelled to 4,220 the following year, but in 1967 slumped back to 2,032, and only 897 in 1968. The final eleven cars were shifted in Italy in 1969, long after the OSI factory had replaced cars with printing equipment manufacture. Reportedly, build quality was never top notch, and less than three dozen survive today. A few Torinos were sold in the Benelux countries, with some even assembled in Belgium, but the new Ford of Europe had launched the highly capable Escort in 1967, and parochial enterprises like the Anglia Torino became redundant. Unlike Filmer M. Paradise himself, who was headhunted by the British Motor Corporation in 1966 and played a key role in the early years of British Leyland.

1964 GM RUNABOUT

On, dear; this one speaks volumes for the male-dominated 1960s car industry. The Runabout was specially designed for women and to be mall-friendly, with its two shopping trolleys that stowed in the back and a three-wheeled layout that was supposed to give 180-degree steering manoeuvrability. It was in the GM Futurama display at the 1964 New York World's Fair.

1964 TRIUMPH FURY

In a time long before the Triumph Stag, this two-seater with bodywork by Michelotti was envisaged as a unitary-construction sports car to replace the separate-chassis TR4A. The single prototype built has 2.0-litre Vitesse-type six-cylinder power and features two-part concealed headlights. It is cherished by its current owner, collector Jane Weitzmann.

Above: The fifth-generation Super Snipe, a luxury car that didn't stick around very long.

Opposite: The 2.2-litre Humber Hawk was identified by its single headlights.

1964 HUMBER HAWK MKIV & SUPER SNIPE MKV

There's an end-of-the-pier melancholy to contemplating the last of the big Humbers; another bit of traditional, post-colonial Britain that quietly crumbled away. This pair were the final new versions announced by the old-established Coventry-based marque of Humber, long part of the nation's motoring fabric. Harold Wilson personally owned a Super Snipe, and they were familiar from Whitehall to town hall, and in business circles, outside far-away embassies and even in police car livery. Yet nobody seemed much bothered when the parent Rootes Group quietly announced there'd be no more of them.

These big saloons (and, soon after, big estates) were launched in 1957. The principal advance over outgoing models was integral chassis-body monocoque construction, at the time the biggest such car structure manufactured in the UK. The Hawk used a 2.2-litre four-cylinder engine, with a three-speed manual gearbox controlled from an undesirable column gear change. The more upmarket Super Snipe ran a 2.6-litre six-cylinder, although it lacked much oomph. Both could be had with overdrive, automatic transmission, and a capacious estate car body style.

Rootes tinkered constantly to buoy customer interest, adding the UK's first quad-headlamp design to what was, in essence, an overall profile inspired by mid-1950s Chevrolet sedans. Front disc brakes were added too, and the Super Snipe really benefitted from an engine boost to 3.0 litres that gave it 124bhp of power to equal its quite lavish leather cabin, and occasionally brush 100mph.

Finally, as here, in 1964 the styling was overhauled with a six-light side window design and deeper windscreen, and a rear anti-roll bar aimed to improve the pitching, sloppy handling. Optional power steering, and always a three-speed manual (although most Snipes were autos anyway), conspired to offer little stimulation for the driver, but of course the car was pretty comfy to be chauffeured in. And regally stable on motorways, too. Right at the very end of the production run there was also a range-topping Imperial with a black vinyl roof as a tepid response to Ford's Executive and Vauxhall's Viscount.

The Hawk MkIV and Snipe MkV were very sluggish sellers, with fewer than 3,000 shifted per year on average. They were also-rans to everything from the Ford Zodiac to the Rover 3-litre and, while a Mercedes-Benz saloon was in another league cost-wise, it was superior in every respect to the lumbering Humbers.

In 1964, the year they were unveiled, the American Chrysler Corporation bought into the Rootes Group as part of its international expansion, acquiring a 30 per cent shareholding that they upped to 45 per cent a year later. By 1967 it owned the whole shebang. In all that time it could have green-lit new big Humbers yet never did, instead commanding Rootes to import the Australian-made Chrysler Valiant and retail that as a replacement. Valiants were duly displayed at the London Motor Show in October 1968. Coming from Australia, naturally they had right-hand drive, but were American-style cars with huge six- and V8-cylinder engines – far too big and thirsty to appeal as Humber replacements. British managers at the renamed Chrysler United Kingdom seemed to completely ignore the American head office edict and barely marketed them at all …

Below: One of the later 2.6-litre Debonairs – the car was made for twenty-two years, visually unaltered.

Opposite: A narrow Lincoln Continental? Mitsubishi insisted the Debonair fitted a specific brief.

1964 MITSUBISHI DEBONAIR

The Mitsubishi Group is one of Japan's most influential and longest-established conglomerates. This trading and manufacturing empire is so massive that it represents almost 8 per cent of the revenue of all publicly traded companies there, and at one point in the 1980s accounted for 10 per cent of Japan's entire workforce. It's long been a bastion of national prosperity.

Senior executives, naturally, viewed the 1964 Tokyo Olympics as an opportunity for Mitsubishi to shine, and the impetus to create a prestige car to reflect the Group's standing. It was an unusual undertaking because it would be primarily for the firm's own key figures, rather than retail sale, and intended to be driven only by chauffeurs.

The process began in 1961 by recruiting a German-American General Motors designer seeking a break from Detroit, Hans Bretzner. He was proficient in all the very latest car design techniques and technologies, including prototype modelling, then almost unknown in Japan, and was paired up with the venture's engineering chief, Kensaku Kobayashi.

Bretzner probably didn't anticipate Mitsubishi Motors' insistence that the car must be no more than 1.7m wide, so it qualified as a small car under prevailing regulations. 'This is the worst law under the sun,' he fulminated frequently at the narrow-mindedness, but he was stuck with it. The influential car then for luxury design was the Lincoln Continental, styled by Bretzner's friend Elwood Engel, and that was very broad and flat, so it was challenging to adapt its sharp-edged lines to Mitsubishi's corporate limo. But he succeeded in shaping a very formal and impressive saloon, with a high waistline.

Bretzner was involved in every aspect of it, which included the styling and materials of the interior, and especially the opening rear quarterlights, padded armrests, footwell lighting and radio controls for the crucial, sumptuous back seat. He decamped to a textile factory in Kyoto to create the pearl leather and textured jacquard upholstery. He even suggested two names (Marquis was rejected, Debonair approved) and designed the stand and brochure for the ritzy unveiling at the Tokyo motor show in October 1963, as well as selecting the first Debonair's shimmering pearl white paintjob (Hans made all the paint choices, naturally).

Mitsubishi came up with a brand-new, 2-litre six-cylinder, twin-carburettor engine for the car, which came in a single complete specification, the only choices being a four-speed manual transmission or three-speed Borg Warner automatic. Power was 104bhp, which gave a modest 96mph top speed, but the Debonair was about comfort, and the relatively soft ride certainly gave that.

Excited Mitsubishi top brass received their first deliveries in July 1964. Indeed, they loved their exclusive top-tier car so dearly that it was in production, visually unchanged, until 1986 (the six-cylinder engine was swapped for a 2.6-litre four with automatic gearbox only in 1976). One amusing nickname for the Debonair was the 'running coelacanth' for its latter-day antiquity, its 1960s US-inspired lines looking extremely dated. Around 22,000 examples were sold, every one at a thumping loss. Yet thanks to the work of Hans Bretzner and the Debonair, Mitsubishi's car design abilities became world class in double-quick time.

Above: Big, fast and impeccably hand-finished, here comes the Diplomat V8 coupé.

Opposite: The Diplomat was Chevrolet-derived but Karmann helped make the rare coupé.

1964 OPEL DIPLOMAT

A really large and impressive car with an Opel badge had last been seen in the 1930s. It took almost twenty years after the Second World War for the German subsidiary of General Motors to rebuild its confidence, and indeed its badly bombed facilities, to the point where it could return to top-echelon luxury and power. The country was now booming again, so why should Mercedes-Benz take all the cream?

In February 1964 Opel's 'KAD' series was unveiled, a three-car range of Kapitän, Admiral and Diplomat editions of essentially the same four-door saloon. The firm's recent priorities had been the small Kadett and Rekord cars. There was neither the capacity nor the budget to create a range-topper for the marque from the ground up, but being part of a major multinational solved this issue. Opel was able to use General Motors' so-called 'X-body' rear-wheel drive platform and drivetrain already thoroughly proven in the Chevrolet Chevy II. And while that was regarded as somewhere between a 'compact' and an 'intermediate' size of sedan in the US, for Europe it underpinned a very large saloon indeed.

The Kapitän with 2.6 or 2.8-litre straight-six engines formed the entry-level offering, and quickly became Germany's top-selling six-cylinder car. The Admiral was a step up in prestige, and could in addition be ordered with a Chevrolet-supplied 4.6-litre V8 engine combined with a two-speed Powerglide automatic transmission, power steering and powered all-round disc brakes.

Meanwhile, the Diplomat took its dignified place at the peak of the range, and was offered only with the V8 engine and auto gearbox. It was positively sumptuous inside, with deeply padded leather seats, electric windows front and back, Blaupunkt Köln radio and a two-tone steering wheel neatly colour co-ordinated with the interior trim. The prominent ribbon speedo and T-bar gear shift were pure Detroit, but the overall effect was tasteful.

In 1965 Opel decided to excel itself above and beyond even the Diplomat with a highly exclusive coupé version. The sleek two-door body for this was hand-crafted and exquisitely finished at the Osnabrück coachworks of Karmann, with individual bucket seats in the back and its interior garlanded with real wood trim to dashboard and door panels.

There was a further upgrade under the bonnet because the engine was now straight out of the Chevrolet Corvette, the 5.4-litre 'small-block' V8. This overcame some cooling issues with the original engine at the very high speeds Germany's *autobahns* encouraged and increased power from 220 to 230bhp; the Diplomat coupé became a 125mph car that could hit 62mph from standstill in nine seconds, accompanied by an engine burble that was characteristically American.

At 25,500DM, the Diplomat coupé was incredibly expensive, more even than a Mercedes-Benz S-Class and some seven times dearer than a Volkswagen Beetle. Only 347 were sold among 9,152 Diplomats, and it was axed from the range in 1967; after the Diplomat A gave way to the new B series in 1968 there would be no new large coupé until the Monza in 1978, at which time the directly US-led influence had gone.

Above: The humblest car in this Audi range was this 1.5-litre 60L, introduced in 1968.

Opposite: The Variant estate (this is a 75) accounted for just one in sixteen of F103s, despite its practicality.

1965 AUDI F103 SERIES

This seemingly unremarkable range of family cars is highly significant as the foundation of the mighty Audi the world knows and admires today. This is where it all sprang from.

Audi itself goes back a lot further. The very first car with that name appeared in 1915, and Audi was one of four marques brought together in 1932 to form the Auto Union company, although it went into abeyance for twenty years after the Second World War, when Auto Union only sold DKW cars. The DKW F102 of 1963 was one of these, and its combination of front-wheel drive with a two-stroke, three-cylinder engine could trace its roots back to the early 1930s.

Daimler-Benz, parent company of Mercedes-Benz, acquired the Auto Union business in 1958 when it was at a low ebb and sales were declining. Two-stroke engines were seen as the culprit, as they were old-fashioned, noisy, and prone to both premature wear and unpleasant pollution as they burned through oil in the combustion process. Fortuitously, Daimler-Benz had ready a robust four-stroke, four-cylinder engine it had developed for an abandoned military vehicle project, and fitting that into the F102 – with its nose elongated to accommodate it, as it was mounted longitudinally while still driving the front wheels – proved transformational.

The F103 arrived at the very point Daimler-Benz had a change of heart and decided to sell Auto Union to Volkswagen in 1965. And in trying to make as clean a start as possible, VW opted to revive the Audi name for the new range, while retaining the four-interconnected rings of the old Auto Union logo as a nod to its heritage; all the two-stroke cars were dropped shortly afterwards.

The Audi 72 was the first version, a compact two- or four-door saloon with a 72bhp 1.7-litre engine and, like all F103s, four-speed manual gearbox. In 1966 a three-door Variant estate joined the line-up, as did an 80 model with corresponding power output, and a lushly appointed 1.8-litre Super 90, which could reach 100mph and so was something of a cut-price BMW … and a taste of Audi's performance image to come later. Suspension was by all-round torsion bars, steering was rack and pinion, and front disc brakes were standard.

In 1968 there were more changes, with a smaller 1.5-litre Audi 60 and a more powerful 80 both offered in all body styles. The final change came in 1969 when the 75 replaced the original 72, and the car continued to be offered until 1972, by when 416,853 had been made. Only one in sixteen were Variants, but the feisty Super 90 proved particularly popular with 49,794 sold, of which some 10,000 pioneered the Audi brand in the USA.

These were sound and competent if unremarkable cars, barely recalled today and never really sought after. Where they mattered was in setting the well-resolved template for the future generations of Audi 80s and 100s, as well as the Volkswagen Passat. VW took its time to get all the fundamentals right but the F103 range, via DKW and Mercedes-Benz, underpins it all.

1965 MERCEDES-BENZ 600 2-DOOR

There were just two of these 'personal' versions of the 600, which was usually supplied as a large four-door saloon or huge six-door limousine. They were built on a wheelbase shortened by 220cm as gifts for retiring key staff, including head of research and development Rudolf Fritz Nallinger. Wing vents were for the air-conditioning system. (Mercedes-Benz Classic)

1965 VOLKSWAGEN KARMANN GHIA 1600 FASTBACK

Volkswagen's Type 3 was a series of saloons and estates that also numbered a Karmann Ghia 1500 coupé in its rank. This fastback design was proposed (but rejected) by Karmann as a sporty rendition of the Type 3 1600TL fastback, and has a corresponding long slope to its roof. It survives in the factory collection at Osnabrück, Germany.

Above: The second-generation Corvair had lovely lines, and by 1965 very few bugbears.

Opposite: A fantastic sectional showpiece showed exactly where the Corvair II's heart lay.

1965 CHEVROLET CORVAIR II

'Compacts' typified by the Dodge Lancer (see p. 20) did much to reshape the US car industry in the early 1960s, and the rear-engined Chevrolet Corvair was by far the most technically adventurous with its air-cooled, aluminium, flat-six engine, all-round independent suspension, automatic transmission as standard, clean lines that were highly influential, and even low-profile tyres. The car masterminded by Chevrolet general manager Ed Cole was the 1960 *Motor Trend* magazine Car of the Year for sound reasons. He even called it 'in effect, the American Volkswagen'.

There was even more novelty with the sporty Corvair Monza coupé and convertible in 1962, on which a turbocharged engine was an exciting option. Yet because Corvairs were expensive to make with all their brand-new features, they sold briskly rather than spectacularly. Nor was it particularly economical, unlike the small imported cars whose job it was for the Corvair to repel. Spoilt US consumers were pretty fickle, too; first, in 1962, Chevrolet launched a conventional compact, the Chevy II, to stop buyers defecting to the Ford Falcon, and the massive success (1.5 million sold in its first two years) of the Ford Mustang 'personal' car in 1964 then concentrated all minds on Chevrolet's rival offering, the 1967 Camaro.

Still, Chevrolet had splashed a small fortune positioning the Corvair as the enthusiast's choice in the market, and was not going to give up on it. Designers were tasked with completely revising the car, and for 1965 all new styling arrived with especially sleek and elegant lines, and pillarless side windows in both two- and four-door forms. Engines were uprated, offering power from 110 to 180bhp, and the rear suspension was completely redesigned with Corvette components to counter handling that some drivers had found to be wayward on slippery roads.

The previous Corvair's best year was 1961 when 337,000 were sold, so when the second generation shifted 247,000 in 1965, the omens still looked good. Unfortunately, though, things were about to turn ugly.

Consumer rights campaigner Ralph Nader (later he also ran for the US presidency) published his book *Unsafe at Any Speed* in 1965. His opening chapter contained a searing criticism of General Motors for cynically allowing the Corvair to reach showrooms while knowing it had safety drawbacks, relating to the 1960–63 rear suspension, and the car's propensity to spin. He drew on evidence in 100 lawsuits from Corvair drivers who'd crashed, and although later reports concluded the Corvair in fact was no more likely to suffer loss of control than any similar car in extreme conditions, the reputational damage was devastating. It was in no way helped by GM's surly response to the crisis.

In 1966 sales had collapsed by more than 50 per cent and, with everyone's focus on knobbling the Mustang, all Corvair development programmes, advertising campaigns and motor racing support were cancelled. No one, it seemed, was interested in hearing about what a very well-sorted car the Corvair II now was. Chevrolet stuck by it for three more years to appear undefeated, but sales were pitiful: they shrank from 27,000 in 1967 (final year for the four-door sedan) to just 6,000 for 1969 when, on 14 May, the last Corvair was built. They've long been sought after as collectable cars, and the Corvair II is a firm fan favourite.

Left: Hello, sunny: both 204 convertible and, in the distance, 204 coupé were chic cars.

Opposite: The all-new, front-wheel drive 204 saw the small car market bloom for Peugeot.

1965 PEUGEOT 204

How can France's No. 1 bestseller for three successive years in 1969–71 qualify for this book, you might reasonably ask. With 1.6 million examples sold up to 1976, the Peugeot 204 can hardly be called arcane, and while very few remain functional and roadworthy, that's normal in a small family car last on sale half a century ago.

Nevertheless, the 204 and its excellent qualities lie strangely uncared for where similar models from rival manufacturers continually gather warm and nostalgic tributes. There are two main reasons for this indifference. But, first, to this car's strongpoints.

It was totally new from nose to tail, quite something from a deeply conservative organisation like Peugeot; it had last offered a small car in 1949, but this renaissance was rich in innovation. The 204 was Peugeot's first front-wheel drive car, also featuring a transversely mounted engine with a four-speed, all-synchromesh gearbox tucked beneath it like a BMC Mini or 1100. The single overhead-camshaft four-cylinder engine of 1130cc was developed from scratch, and cast aluminium throughout. The neat four-door, five-seater saloon body was styled by Pininfarina, and shortly after launch came an estate, a delivery van, and both a hatchback coupé and a very pretty convertible.

In 1967, *Motor Sport* magazine drove one in Britain, where because of import duties it cost £903 against £835 for a more opulent and powerful Triumph 1300. 'I regard it as one of the most significant small cars of the nineteen-sixties,' cooed the reporter. 'In comparison, other fwd 1100s feel and sound like – tramcars …' He went on to applaud the 204's supple coil-spring, all-independent suspension, fast cornering on grippy Michelin X tyres – despite heeling over alarmingly with tyres squealing – its excellent steering and front disc/rear drum brakes, safe handling, refined engine and comfy seats.

Hard to stomach, for the UK price (not so galling in France, then) was the grimly uninviting interior, with hard-wearing plastic upholstery, vinyl headlining, and rubber floor covering. There was no glovebox or door pockets, no opening quarterlights, minimal instruments and switches on a spartan dashboard, and a column-mounted gear lever. Weekly magazine *Autocar* adjudged the interior 'austere and disappointing'.

With overall fuel consumption of 36mph, the 204 was economical but, with just 53bhp, hard work was required to reach its happy cruising lick of 70mph. An estate with a 1255cc diesel engine – introduced in 1968, and the smallest diesel production car of its day – gave a miserly 50mpg, but was even slower.

This question of speed was the car's other downside, especially for rallying. Shekhar Mehta, a rising rally star, was offered a 204 for the 1968 and '69 East African Safari Rallies because Peugeot was keen to promote it there, where its larger cars already sold well. 'It suited the rallies in Uganda where there weren't any big hills and sharp bends, so I was quite pleased with it,' he recalled in an interview in *Motor Sport* magazine in August 1998. 'The worst thing was the car was so painfully slow. It would only do 82mph. Mechanically the Peugeot was sound but its destiny was as a shopping car. All I can say is it taught you patience.'

Left: A GT40 tackling the traffic madness of Piccadilly Circus – an easy job after Le Mans.

Opposite: Extra headlights and many other changes were needed to equip the GT40 for the road.

1966 FORD GT40 MKIII

In 1962, Henry Ford II offered to buy Ferrari, to add racing glamour to the gigantic business his grandfather founded. Ford glory in the Le Mans 24 Hours race was his goal, and so when Enzo Ferrari wouldn't capitulate, Ford decided to build his own car and give the Italians a pasting. Coincidentally, British racing car constructor Lola had just completed its promising, mid-engined Mk6 GT using a Ford V8 engine. So an opportune Ford snapped up this project and engaged Lola founder Eric Broadley to turn it into the Ford GT40 – so-called because it was only 40in tall.

At Le Mans in 1965 Ferrari won and Phil Hill's GT40 retired with gearbox damage, but not before setting a new lap record of 3 minutes 49.2 seconds – averaging 131.37mph. A redesigned GT40 proceeded to win at Le Mans four times: 1966–69. The first victory with Bruce McLaren and Chris Amon also saw the GT40 become the first car to cover 3,000 miles in the race. By 1967 Ford retired, mission completed, but a private team took the two other Le Mans wins using the very same GT40. In 1969, Jacky Ickx beat Hans Herrmann's Porsche by a photo-finish 120m. The GT40's reputation in endurance sports car racing was sealed.

From the organisation founded on 15 million Model Ts, unsurprisingly Ford couldn't contain its quest for sales. It had always intended to sell road-going GT40s. That's why it insisted on a cheap steel monocoque structure rather than Broadley's far lighter aluminium 'tub', and dictated the body styling, which compromised aerodynamics at race speeds.

The MkIII was the dedicated GT40 road car, significantly altered for its new role. This included an extended tail for luggage space, repositioning the gear lever (for the balky ZF five-speeder) between body-hugging, leather-upholstered seats, and raising ground clearance and adding two extra headlamps to meet US lighting laws. In addition there were softer shock absorbers, masses of polyurethane sound deadening, opening side windows and even an ashtray. Gleaming Borrani wire wheels were fitted.

The engine was an all-iron 4.7-litre Ford V8, similar to the fearsome Shelby Mustang GT350's, detuned from almost 500bhp to 306bhp at 5,000rpm, with maximum torque at 329lb ft at 4,200rpm, to meet legal emissions levels. With an estimated 165mph top speed and 5.3-second 0–60mph acceleration this was – according to your bravery levels – the most thrilling or alternatively terrifying road-going car anywhere. Your pockets needed to be goldmine-deep too: the stated US price of $18,500 would have paid for seven Ford Mustangs.

For that you got astonishingly bad quality. *Car & Driver* magazine in June 1967 was frank: 'The workmanship and most of the hardware in this, the most costly Ford of all, are miserably below the standards of the meanest Falcon. Most of what's wrong happened in the translation from racer to street machine. It's about as reliable as a $2 watch … everything except the ignition circuit would cut out at unpredictable moments.'

The car wasn't a success. Seven were built in four years, with only three paying customers: Max Aitken Jnr, chairman of the *Daily Express* newspaper, Austrian conductor Herbert von Karayan, and Florida's Joseph Chandler, whose car came with tinted glass and air conditioning.

Above: The brochure cover for the all-new six-cylinder Genie indicated its Welsh heritage.

Opposite: The Genie was well-engineered and handsome, the equal of many mainstream cars.

1966 GILBERN GENIE

The Gilbern story is a wonderful capsule of the life of a specialist British car marque, rooted in passion and, although just over 1,000 were sold in total, still much treasured by an owner community today. It remains the only significant car company ever based in Wales.

It all started when butcher GILes Smith from Pontypridd met engineer BERNard Friese, originally from Germany and a Second World War prisoner-of-war who'd stayed on to make his life in Britain. Giles declared he fancied building a kit car, but Bernard persuaded him he could design something far superior from scratch, and in 1959 he did just that. The Gilbern GT turned out so well they jointly decided to become manufacturers because no other small GTs were available in the UK. Bernard's square-tube chassis frame carried an attractive two-plus-two-seater fastback body, and cleverly used off-the-shelf parts: 948cc BMC A series engine, Austin A35 front suspension, and Morris Minor back axle, well located with twin trailing arms and coil springs. Once the two got cracking, selling one car a week, further engine choices included 1.6-litre MGA and 1.5 Coventry Climax.

Glowing write-ups in magazines reeled in customers, and the partners settled on supplying the car not as a kit – for which the buyer had to hunt down his own mechanical parts – but in complete 'component' form with everything included, brand new and guaranteed, and zero-rated for Purchase Tax (the VAT of its day). It simply required the customer to install, or have installed, the drivetrain, connect everything up, and turn the key. Even a skilled mechanic found this would take longer than the single weekend Gilbern brightly suggested!

By 1965 they presided over a neat factory in the Rhondda Valley and were accepted as a bona fide carmaker by the Society of Motor Manufacturers & Traders. And at this point they upped their game with a brand-new car in 1966, the Genie.

It was a much more accomplished four-seater GT now powered by 2.5- or 3.0-litre V6 Ford engines, and suspension and rear axles mostly from the MGB. Wire wheels, and then alloys, were standard, as were twin fuel tanks, with electric windows optional. Some 90 per cent of Genies were sold in component form.

The company was acquired in 1968 by a local maker of pub fruit machines called Ace Group (not to be confused with Ace Motor Co., Gilbern's London dealer), and after 197 Genies had been made the car was renamed the Invader in 1970, with many detail improvements and upmarket touches. The founders had run their business on a shoestring, often hand building the cars themselves, but new investment, extra staff and increased production didn't bring more profits. Genies and Invaders were generally rated well by contemporary writers, despite some rough edges and a firm ride quality. The company couldn't outrun the early 1970s fuel crisis, however, and the last Gilbern was made in 1974, by which time VAT was applied to home-build cars and so sales suffered. Surviving cars are much cherished by the Gilbern Owners' Club, founded in 1969, and with so many components shared with mainstream production models, keeping them going is relatively easy.

1966 FERRARI 365P BERLINETTA SPECIALE

A very long time before Ferrari's Berlinetta Boxer came this Pininfarina prototype at the Paris motor show, the first with a 4.4-litre V12 engine mounted in the middle of the car, and so a potential Lamborghini Miura counterpart. Just two were built with three-abreast seating, one of them for Fiat supremo Gianni Agnelli.

1966 ASTON MARTIN DBSC

First shown at the Paris motor show in 1966 and dubbed the '170mph Car', Carrozzeria Touring of Milan – despite being in receivership – designed it to succeed the Aston DB6, but ultimately it was shelved in favour of the all-British DBS. This, a second example with left-hand drive, was sold to a private customer. (Tim Scott)

Above: The Mexico was Maserati's ultra-luxurious GT alternative to a Ferrari 365 GT 2+2.

Opposite: Huge exhaust pipes were there to broadcast the bark from a 4.2- or 4.7-litre V8 engine.

1966 MASERATI MEXICO

The curious roots of this elegant and exclusive Maserati help explain its name.

Mexican president Adolfo Lopez Mateos had treated himself to a Maserati 5000 GT with a body by Italian coachbuilder Allemano in 1961, but when the left-wing land reformer tired of his expensive plaything it was sold to fellow countryman Diez Barroso. Before long the car was damaged in a major road accident, after which it was shipped back to Maserati in Modena, Italy for repair.

Completely separately, another coachbuilder – Vignale – had displayed a glamorous prototype for a luxury GT on its stand at the 1965 Turin motor show. Code-named Tipo AM122 and built on the shortened chassis of the Maserati Quattroporte four-door luxury saloon, the reaction was so overwhelmingly enthusiastic that plans were immediately made to add the car to the Maserati range.

When Señor Barroso turned up at Modena to discuss his car's rejuvenation, he caught sight of the AM122 prototype in the workshops and decided he wanted that even more than his repaired 5000 GT. Reportedly, he had the 5000 GT chassis number transferred to the prototype so that it could be returned home without any customs duties to pay! In all of this, 'Maserati Mexico' became the title of the new production car … a decision that paid off wonderfully when, and co-incidentally, John Surtees won the 1966 Mexican Grand Prix in a Cooper-Maserati F1.

The final customer-ready version, artfully shaped by Vignale's in-house designer Virginio Vairo, was previewed at the 20th International Concours d'Elegance in Rimini on 6 August 1966, before an official public unveiling at the Paris motor show that October. Maserati now had a fabulous new competitor to the Aston Martin DB6, Ferrari 365 GT 2+2, Iso Rivolta and Jensen Interceptor.

The power unit was Maserati's race-bred (from the 450S sports car) 4.7-litre V8, developing a mighty 290bhp in a Quattroporte chassis with a wheelbase 4.3in shorter. Alongside it was a 260bhp 4.2-litre edition, which could reach a 142mph top speed against the hotter car's 155. It was anticipated that most buyers would want the five-speed ZF manual transmission, but a three-speed Borg Warner automatic was also offered, and a mere twenty-two lazy customers chose that. The standard Borrani wire wheels fronted Maserati's first use of twin-servo ventilated disc brakes.

While most enthusiasts would be drooling at the under-bonnet vista, the four-seater accommodation boasted its own gorgeousness, beautifully leather-trimmed and with a polished mahogany dashboard supporting gleaming chrome-edged dials. Air conditioning and electric windows were included as standard, and the only other options besides the auto were power steering and your choice of radio.

Any mature and self-respecting playboy would have wanted one, and the Mexico sold well, with 300 4.2s and 180 4.7s delivered. But with its subtle, urbane looks it was quite a low-profile car – in striking contrast to Maserati's more overtly sporty Ghibli and Mistral. It was replaced by the Maserati Indy in 1972. In the UK, at least, no wonder the car is hardly known at all; there were only nine Mexicos with right-hand drive.

The Peel VIKING-SPORT G.T. CAR BODY

Manufacturers:
Peel Engineering Ltd.,
Viking Works, Isle of Man.

will Transform your Mini

Above: The Viking Sport brochure showing the finest GT car ever to escape the Isle of Man.

Opposite: All you needed was £230, a scrap Mini and lots of spare time to build this yourself.

1966 PEEL VIKING SPORT GT

The Viking wasn't so much a car as a car-shaped replacement part. Its price of £230 was extremely cheap, and all you received in return was a plastic monocoque bodyshell bonded to a square-tube chassis frame, with almost nothing else except a set of instructions.

By the mid-1960s there was a growing pile of written-off Minis across Britain, mangled in accidents to the point that the bodywork was beyond rescue. Scrapyards were groaning with them, and in among this twisted debris lay opportunity. Isle of Man boatbuilder Cyril Cannell was a man with plenty of experience working with glass fibre, not just for waterborne craft but for his Peel three-wheeled microcars; including the P50 that Jeremy Clarkson made globally famous by driving one through the BBC *Top Gear* offices. After these failed to catch on in the 1960s, Cyril designed the Viking as a way to breathe new life into those Mini wrecks.

There were kit cars before and after Cyril's effort, but few made such a virtue of recycling absolutely everything from the donor car (or van, as the Viking adopted the van's longer wheelbase) – one that could be bought for a song from any breaker's yard. Indeed, because the Mini's engine, transmission, steering, front and rear subframes and suspension, wheels, glass, seats, lights and all the dashboard dials and switchgear were reused, the Viking counted as simply a replacement body, and the original car's legal identity and registration number were retained. Everything just transferred over, and Cyril even made glass fibre cut-down copies of the Mini's doors so old windows, locks and inner door trim/bins could be installed.

With its cheeky frontal styling and built-in rear airdam, you ended up with a cute and distinctive little fastback GT for minimal cost, even though there was no longer an opening boot – luggage had to be stuffed in behind the old Mini's back seat.

It caused a stir at the 1966 Racing Car Show in London's Olympia. Before Cyril Cannell had really supplied any, he decided to sell the project (concentrating on moulding motorcycle fairings instead) to entrepreneur Bill Last of Suffolk who, without the choppy barrier of the Irish Sea to overcome, was much better placed to sell Vikings than Peel Engineering. He established Viking Performance Ltd to do just that, and renamed the car the Viking Minisport. But in three years until 1970 Last is thought to have sold just twenty-two more examples after he changed tack to become deeply involved with the Trident Clipper (see p. 118). The Viking was quickly sidelined.

The key reason for its pathetic sales performance was ferocious competition from the Mini Marcos, which already had the Marcos image and reputation to draw on. The timing was unfortunate, too, as the Mini Marcos made its debut at the same Racing Car Show in January 1966, offering an almost identical concept but at an even leaner £199. Within six months, a plucky Mini Marcos had amazed everyone by completing the Le Mans 24 Hours race, finishing an unbelievable fifteenth overall, and sales soared, leaving the Viking to forlornly fade away.

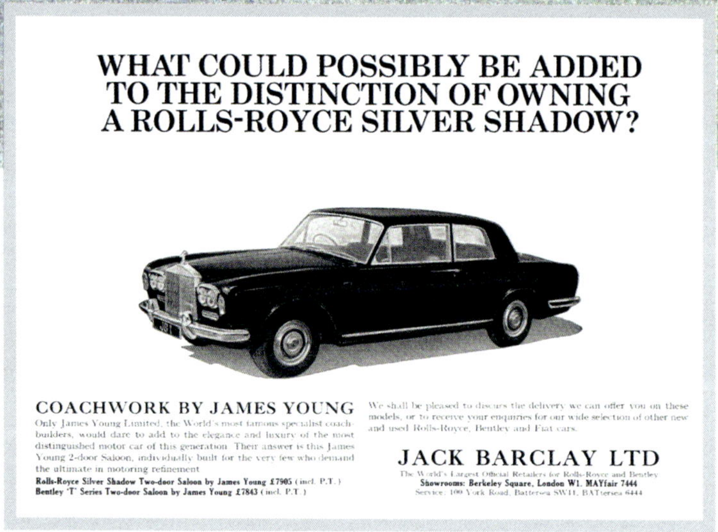

Above: Keep looking and eventually it dawns that this Bentley T-Series only has two doors.

Right: Jack Barclay's advert extolling the virtues of the James Young Rolls Shadow conversion.

WHAT COULD POSSIBLY BE ADDED TO THE DISTINCTION OF OWNING A ROLLS-ROYCE SILVER SHADOW?

COACHWORK BY JAMES YOUNG

JACK BARCLAY LTD

1966 ROLLS-ROYCE SILVER SHADOW & BENTLEY T SERIES 2-DOOR SALOON

Luxury cars flourished in the 1960s, but the long-established 'carriage trade' did not. Britain's upper-echelon coachbuilding houses – many had transitioned from the horse-drawn era of the late 1800s – were now ailing. The reason was obvious. For some sixty years, upmarket car manufacturers had mostly made only separate chassis, leaving the bodywork to outside coachwork firms. Once their cars came as a single welded structure, with chassis and body integrated, the coachbuilder's contribution was no longer needed.

Not even the highly upstanding Rolls-Royce was immune to this progress. In 1965 the Silver Shadow replaced the Silver Cloud, and so a modern monocoque unit usurped the robust rolling chassis with separate panels. It was a vastly superior car in its integrity, handling, refinement and safety, but customisation opportunities shrank to paintwork, upholstery and electric accessories. A Silver Cloud buyer could have ordered it in chassis-only form and then selected a body style, and a coachbuilder, to complete a one-off. Not any longer.

One independent coachbuilder valiantly upheld tradition: James Young & Co., in business in Bromley, Kent, since 1863. It had been acquired in 1937 by London Rolls-Royce and Bentley dealer Jack Barclay, and henceforth its craft was devoted exclusively to those two celebrated marques, especially its Bentley Continental sports saloons and Rolls Phantom V limousines, although such cars could be ordered through other Rolls dealers too.

The Silver Shadow, and near-identical Bentley T Series, threatened all this, and so – with full Rolls-Royce approval – James Young set about making a unique iteration: a two-door saloon. The design, James Young's last, was by AF 'Mac' McNeil, whose experience stretched back to the 1930s but, as he died in 1965, he never did see the final car. There being no separate frame, much grinding and welding was required on a bare shell supplied by Rolls-Royce, rather than traditional panel beating from scratch. The rear doors were removed and rear wings extended to meet the front doors, elongated to permit easy access to the rear seats, from which the conversion robbed no legroom. The drivetrain, 6.2-litre V8 engine, automatic transmission and braking system were untouched, but the rear windows now only popped open for ventilation.

Following this brutal metalwork surgery, James Young's coach painters and trimmers could complete the car to the buyer's precise liking of colour and interior. Unique door handles were fitted and, unlike for the regular four-door, there were no full-body-length chrome strips. Otherwise, the car's profile and wheelbase remained unaltered, so it was hard to even tell at a glance that it wasn't a standard Shadow or T. The JY Shadow cost £7,905, a hefty increase over the £6,557 four-door.

In two years James Young produced just fifty of these, fifteen of them Bentleys, before admitting it was futile, and closed down. No one knows how many survive. The conversion made little sense because losing two doors made it far less practical. And the existence of the Silver Shadow coupé and convertible (later renamed Corniche) from Rolls-Royce's own in-house coachbuilder H.J. Mulliner didn't help, especially as those cars' attractively undulating wing line surely rendered them a lot more distinctive.

Above: The Sonett II, the first front-wheel drive small sports car to really get anywhere.

Opposite: An early Sonett II showing the stumpy tail of its all-plastic body.

1966 SAAB SONETT II & V4

Probably the first two-seater sports car with front-wheel drive to meet commercial success, Saab's Sonett II made a bold grab for the US market. As indicated by its name, there had been a Sonett I, a two-seater roadster first seen in 1956 that never progressed beyond prototypes. With the II, Saab got serious. Curiously, though, the origins of the car arose outside the company.

Two engineers, Björn Karlström and Björn Andreasson, had decided to build an all-Swedish sports car using off-the-shelf Saab components, and secured a manufacturing agreement with light aircraft firm Malmö Flygindustri (MFI), which liked their plans. The project was named MFI13, apparently as the number 13 would never be used on a plane because of pilots' superstitions. The first two-seater fastback came together in 1964 with a steel body from which a glass fibre mould was taken to manufacture plastic copies. Power came from Saab's rally-proven three-cylinder, two-stroke 0.8-litre with triple carburettors. Coupled with a highly aerodynamic shape, this gave excellent acceleration of 0–62mph in just 13.7 seconds, and a 93mph top speed.

Saab itself kept tabs on the venture and, when MFI failed to win a crucial government grant, Saab stepped in and bought the whole outfit. Renamed Saab 97, or Sonett II, it only took six more months to put the car on sale, although the first twenty-eight examples were totally (and gingerly) built by hand in late 1966. It had a sleeker, extended nose section, the whole of which tilted forward to access the 60bhp engine.

From the 259th car onwards, the smoky two-stroke engine was replaced by a 1.5-litre vee-four-cylinder from the Ford Taunus, which meant the car complied with more stringent US emissions regulations, was less hard work to drive, and underwent a slight name change. This Sonett V4 was quicker and more powerful but needed an asymmetrical bonnet bulge to house its taller power unit, skewing the looks from quirky to awkward. Nonetheless, these cars put up spirited showings in US sports car races against Austin-Healey Sprites and Triumph Spitfires, and the Sonett V4 became a minor cult. It was great fun to drive, and well sorted over time.

It was a tight fit inside. At first there wasn't even a glovebox lid, which meant the contents often spilled out under hard acceleration. Early cars had a dashboard fronted in plywood with a mahogany-effect stain, later changed to a sportier matt-black crackle finish.

In all, just 1,968 Sonett IIs were built before a major overhaul turned it into the redesigned Sonett III, now with manually operated pop-up headlights and low speed impact-proof bumpers to satisfy more US rules; most Sonett IIs, V4s and IIIs went to North America – there were no right-hand drive cars. Sonett IIs already had three-point seatbelts and a built-in rollbar, while high-backed bucket seats to counteract whiplash and a padded steering wheel had been added in 1969.

From 1970 to 1974 the Sonett III sold well in the US but, sadly and inexplicably Saab never again ventured into the sports car market.

1966 DUESENBERG

This imposing limousine was the result of a failed attempt to revive the 1920s American marque Duesenberg, backed by property tycoon Fred McManis. Unveiled in New York, its extravagant, faux-classic design came from ex-Chrysler stylist Virgil Exner, using a 7.2-litre V8 Chrysler drivetrain, and this one and only prototype was constructed in Italy by Ghia.

1966 VAUXHALL XVR

The XVR was not what you'd expect from Vauxhall in Luton, UK. It was a way-out coupé with gullwing doors that, starting in Geneva in 1966, did a long motor show tour. The styling was by American Wayne Cherry and Brit David Jones, and was meant to show there was real creativity bubbling away inside the British General Motors outpost.

Above: The MBX was a defiant 'image' car for Škoda in the grim Soviet era.

Opposite: In the back was a durable four-cylinder engine, copying Fiat and Renault.

1966 ŠKODA 1000 MBX DE LUXE

Czechoslovakia was a proud and imaginative engineering innovator, and one gets the sense that this irked the country's repressive Russian overlords from the late 1940s to the collapse of the Soviet Union in 1990. In fact, it probably unnerved Moscow, in case technical breakthroughs somehow stoked rebellion.

In car making, for example, Škoda was obliged to turn out basic transport for the workers. Yet, while toiling under this kind of edict, the envelope-pushing types at the Mladá Boleslav factory did all they could to keep up with developments in the decadent West.

The Škoda 1000 MB of 1964 was a good example. In concept it followed the trend-setting strategy of leading European companies Volkswagen, Fiat and Renault in featuring a rear-mounted engine to maximise passenger space, while Škoda devised an innovative four-cylinder engine to boost fuel economy, with a weight-saving aluminium block, a cast iron head for durability, and various high-pressure die castings in its gearbox and crankcase. Many years later Škodas became the butt of jokes; it followed some alarm over dangerous handling if driven incautiously on slippery roads, but really stemmed from the cars' bargain basement status that was a result of Soviet-imposed 'dumping' at artificially low prices.

And in great contrast to the coarse nature of Russia's Ladas, Poland's Polski-Fiats and East Germany's Trabants, Škoda always tried to inject some verve into its affairs, such as with this natty pillarless coupé, which it called the 1000 MBX De Luxe. While the standard 1000 MB was intended as routine family transport, the MBX epitomised the sort of carefree frivolity seemingly incompatible with life behind the Iron Curtain.

The reverse-rake rear screen pillars accommodated a wraparound back window, while all the frameless side windows could be wound down for cruising on warm and sunny days, still with seating for five as in the four-door, and delightfully airy views out; ideal for enjoying the fresh air of, say, the Tatra mountains. The car was revealed at the Geneva motor show in March 1966, signalling its status as a booster for Škoda's image worldwide. And it was assembled in a quiet corner of the plant on a dedicated production line. They were labour-intensive to make, pretty much hand-crafted.

Power came from a 1.0-litre twin-carburettor engine with 52bhp that, because the car weighed just 816kg (1,799lb), delivered excellent fuel economy and a lively enough 79mph top speed. Then in November 1967, the motor was uprated to 1.1-litre for the 1100 MBX De Luxe, with an identical power output but a 7 per cent increase in torque to give better acceleration for overtaking, a more powerful oil pump and improved cooling. Still, these cars continued to be made in tiny numbers: when the MBX was quietly axed in 1969 (and replaced by the S110R) there were 1,403 1000s and 1,114 1100s; a total of 2,517 MBXs beside a whopping 443,156 four-door MB saloons. It was clearly not popular as an export (more than half the cars made were shipped abroad), and within Škoda's homeland even this modest show of automotive exuberance would have got you noticed for the wrong reasons. Rare and quite sought after now.

Above: The Unipower GT aimed to give the excitement of the Ford GT40 at a fraction of the cost.

Opposite: One of the very first production Unipower GTs, its tiny dimensions very obvious. (Tim Carpenter)

1966 UNIPOWER GT

This book scoops up several cars created outside the motoring mainstream, and without the backing and capital of large industry players. None is quite as remarkable as this one, though – an attempt to give adept drivers the full Lamborghini Miura experience in miniature, and at relatively cheap cost.

Ex-Lotus engineer Ernie Unger came up with it, ably helped by his designer friend Ron Bradshaw. Both worked for Ford, and Ron was actually part of the GT40 programme when Ernie mapped out his lightweight, aerodynamic two-seater with a transverse mid-mounted engine, using as many existing parts as possible.

In his own, square-tube chassis he opted for Mini Cooper engines and transmissions, the gear lever mounted on the driver's door side and connected via a specially designed linkage. The glass fibre body definitely had pint-sized Ford GT40 overtones with those cooling intakes behind the doors, and of course a height of just 40.5in. Radiator, spare wheel and fuel tank were crammed under the low bonnet, which gave a front/rear weight (a mere 508kg, or 1,120lb, in total) distribution ratio of an ideal 45:55. This, coupled with the strong structure, gave exceptional handling and grip on dinky alloy wheels.

Unger's pal Tim Powell owned engineering company Universal Power Drives, and being quite a speed freak himself he decided to buy the project. So assembly took place in his Unipower factory in Perivale, Middlesex. Other firms made the chassis frame and body, the instruments, interior trim and reclining bucket seats, and a novel Jack Knight five-speed gearbox was available.

At up to £1,195, a Unipower GT wasn't cheap, although for such an exciting, unusual machine it was, if anything, underpriced. The launch was at the January 1966 Racing Car Show at London's Olympia, where it was the absolute star among road cars, outshining the Peel Viking (see p. 90) and Mini Marcos.

Powell was obsessed with powerboat racing by 1968, and Ernie Unger was forced to find a new backer, which he did in 22-year-old playboy aristocrat Piers Weld-Forester, who had a large inheritance and a thirst for excitement. Assembly shifted to new premises in Park Royal, north London, and the new patron embarked on a motor racing spree in 1969. This took him and driver chums all over Europe and a lot of fun was had, but predictably this drained the company of the necessary cashflow to fulfil orders on its always healthy waiting list. Weld-Forrester constantly interrupted manufacture to work on his racing cars to the dismay of Ernie Unger, whose priority was delivering Unipowers to his paying customers. So it was a very gloomy day when the company was wound up on 19 January 1970 after no more than 75 Unipower GTs had been delivered, twenty-four of them with left-hand drive. Another fantastic British specialist car kyboshed by the harsh reality of business. Fortunately most still exist, and several are still raced … although Ernie Unger did say later (www.unipowergt.uk): 'It was intended as a road car which might be good enough for the occasional amateur sprint. It came as a surprise to be so well received that people wanted to race it seriously.'

Above: The Queen had one of these, although that's not her in the 6ft 4in load bay …

Opposite: The regular Cresta was a 3.3-litre saloon popular with businessmen.

1966 VAUXHALL CRESTA PC ESTATE

The Queen had one of these very rare cars. Yes, Her Majesty Queen Elizabeth II was keen on the biggest Vauxhalls, having been an unlikely yet very satisfied owner of a Cresta PA Friary estate car since 1961. She is said to have consulted closely on its 'country life' specification, and it featured roof-mounted fishing rod carriers, a gun rack, and a hefty dog guard. This car was specially painted in dark Imperial green and carried the jokey registration number MYT 1, and it survives to this day in the royal garage at the Sandringham estate.

While skipping the Cresta PB, the Windsors were back for a Cresta PC estate in August 1967, which once again was a special order in the same colour with all the same custom features, and another great private plate: PYN 1F. What became of the car isn't known, and there are very few photos of it in period; but for a short spell before the Queen had her first Range Rover, it was a part of the Royal Family's precious leisure time.

Such an esteemed customer, however, did nothing to salvage the PC estate's fortunes. The saloon model made its debut in 1965, a large car with a very Americanised aura and a 3.3-litre straight-six under a broad and impressive expanse of bonnet, putting its 123bhp to the road via the rear wheels and a choice of three-speed manual (with column change) or two-speed Powerglide automatic.

The standard PC Cresta had a bench front seat and single headlamps, while the De Luxe came with separate front bucket seats and four headlights, and a much more luxurious interior. Announced in September was the estate version in De Luxe spec only, at £1,507, and the first deliveries were in January 1967.

Vauxhall was so uncommitted to this estate that the car was actually modified by the firm that made Dormobile camper vans, Martin Walter Ltd, at its Folkestone coachworks. It always came with a full warranty from the Luton factory, and was sold through Vauxhall dealers.

The car featured an elongated glass fibre roof and new tailgate, plus additional rear side windows, all of which looked like the afterthoughts they were when tacked on to the trendy 'Coke bottle' profile of the base car. This added 2.5in to the Cresta's height. There was also heavy-duty rear suspension and bigger rear tyres to cope with heavy cargo. The carpeted load platform was 47in long, which increased to an impressive 76in – that's a double-bed size 6ft 4in – when the back seat was folded down. There was a tool box under the floor and the spare wheel stood upright in the back under its own vinyl cover, while an extra wing mirror was also provided.

Despite being the largest estate car made anywhere in Europe in its day, there proved to be few takers. No doubt this was because it cost 40 per cent more than the standard saloon, and some £200 more even than for a Humber Super Snipe or Ford Zodiac estate. A tiny number were sold, and it was quietly dropped from the Cresta range by the end of 1968. The Queen's views on the car, meanwhile, were never made public.

Below: Launch day for the original Austin 3-litre, with its TV-screen headlights.

Opposite: The 3-litre was a big, comfortable saloon that was surprisingly good to drive.

1967 AUSTIN 3-LITRE

This huge saloon, intended for high-flying company execs and other prosperous buyers, was a notorious failure, and routinely mocked for its humdrum name. Once you disregarded nebulous issues around prestige, though, it had many solid and interesting qualities.

The 3-litre was, plainly, a victim of bad timing. Austin had had a large and impressive saloon in its line-up since the 1920s, and as the dominant camp within the British Motor Corporation since the group's creation in 1952, it saw no reason to ditch that tradition when replacing the ageing A110 Westminster. A joint enterprise with Rolls-Royce only resulted in the underwhelming Rolls-powered Vanden Plas 4-litre R (with all Rolls and Bentley versions canned) and in 1963 a different approach was taken with the 'ADO 61' project. A new car was planned around the central passenger compartment structure of the upcoming Austin/Morris 1800, with a revised 3-litre six-cylinder power unit, the rear-wheel drive this class of car demanded, and reimagined front and rear ends to make it distinctive.

What started as a cost-conscious approach led to a very prolonged development period. The 3-litre wasn't unveiled until 1967 and then took another year to reach showrooms, with a £1,418 price. During this interlude one of the most controversial attributes, its 'television-shaped' headlights, were changed to four, conventional round ones, while twenty-five pre-production examples were lent to selected customers to gather real-life feedback. Potential buyers were deterred by the austere styling inside and out, the slightly gutless 2.9-litre engine (shared with the MGC), the unattractive dashboard with strip speedo, and of course the Austin name in a sector dominated by Rover.

If you could get past these things, though, it was pretty good to drive. The ride quality was superb, with the 1800's Hydrolastic suspension all-round and a unique self-levelling system at the back; steering was excellent and handling surprisingly nimble; the seating (despite Ambla plastic upholstery) was comfortable; it was enormously spacious and had a huge boot; and there was beautifully finished wood trim inside. It was also one of the first cars fitted with an alternator.

Events of 1968 heaped more misfortune on the 15½ft-long 3-litre. This was the year Leyland Motors and BMC merged to form British Leyland. The huge new conglomerate now made Jaguars, Daimlers, Rovers and Triumphs in excellent large saloon form; there was no room, or love, for Austin's cobbled-together contender. It was too late to cancel the car but it survived three loss-making years as a British Leyland product, during which only 9,992 were sold … against hopelessly optimistic projections of 10,000 cars annually. The last glided out of the Cowley factory in April 1971.

Subsequent decades proved even harsher for 3-litres. They became unwanted second-hand cars that were too thirsty and tricky to maintain for most buyers. Then banger racers discovered how robust and powerful these 125bhp tanks were, and sacrificed hundreds on dirt tracks where they were hammered into blocks of scrap metal – a tragedy for any classic car, but even sadder for an impressive luxury limo that promised, and actually delivered, quite a lot.

1967 FORD COMUTA

One of the slowest cars in this book, at 25mph, was created in Essex, UK, by engineers at Ford as an experiment into electric-powered personal urban transport. The range, on lead-acid batteries, was about 40 miles, hardly impressive, but then these were the early days of electric cars, and the Comuta was a brave buzz.

1967 BERTONE LAMBORGHINI MARZAL

The Bertone Lamborghini Marzal was one of the most recognisable concept cars of the 1960s, partly thanks to countless millions of toy cars that captured its dramatic lines and double-glazed, full-length gullwing doors. It made its debut in Geneva in 1967 and was designed by Marcello Gandini. The chassis was from the Miura, with its engine halved to a 2.0-litre straight-six.

Above: Named after a fictional horse, Isuzu's Florian was part of an ingenious range.

Opposite: In its original form, the Florian's Italian lines helped to set it apart.

1967 ISUZU FLORIAN

By the time the unusually proportioned Florian came along, the Kanagawa-based truck company Isuzu had spent fourteen years honing its car craft. The early part of this period involved making Britain's Hillman Minx under licence; it did such an accomplished job that the engineer sent from Coventry to Japan to help, Ken Middleton, confessed that the Isuzu-built cars were better made than the British ones. All that practice led Isuzu to launch its own saloon car, the Bellel, in 1961; a vague facsimile of the Morris Oxford MkV, the Bellel became the first Japanese passenger car offered with a diesel engine. In every other respect, though, it was unmemorable, and Isuzu set about remedying that with Project 117, an all-new range to include a saloon, station wagon, coupé and pick-up.

Rather than amateurishly ape European cars, Isuzu decided to employ a European design house to create new ones, and picked Carrozzeria Ghia. First out of the traps was the 117 Coupé unveiled as a prototype at the 1966 Geneva motor show, a beautiful car styled by a very young Ghia junior called Giorgetto Giugiaro. Next to be unveiled was the Ghia Isuzu 117 Sedan at the Tokyo show shortly afterwards, the work of fellow Ghia artist Filippo Sapino. By the following year's Tokyo event where the production model went on sale, it had been renamed Florian, after the fictional horse in Felix Salten's novel *Florian: The Emperor's Stallion*.

The spacious five-seater Florian had a distinctive semi-fastback body style with three side windows, and was the Bellel's direct replacement. The overhead-valve engine was a 1.6-litre, four-cylinder whose 84bhp went to the rear wheels. A twin-carburettor 1600TS model lifted that to 90bhp in 1969, and very shortly afterwards a new overhead-camshaft engine was introduced. Isuzu said there were thirty-seven different safety features in the car, which also sported a dashboard with oval instruments and pods, and reclining front bucket seats (twin benches were offered on the six-seater estate, confusingly named the 'Van').

Curiously, the 117 pick-up was held back until 1972. General Motors had taken a 34 per cent stake in Isuzu a year earlier and wanted the pick-up for the US market, where it was imported from Japan and sold as the Chevrolet LUV (for Light Utility Vehicle). It was massively successful there, selling 100,000 a year at one stage, and Isuzu then marketed its own version, called the Faster; in the Crewcab version of this, you can easily detect the very same four door panels taken straight from the Florian, all of which explains the car's awkward contours and long wheelbase.

The Ghia lines on the Florian itself were ruined by two clumsy subsequent facelifts, adding ever larger and uglier lights. A 1.8-litre engine was followed later by a diesel option. Sustained by Chevrolet LUV exports, the ageing Florian somehow remained on sale until 1983. Over those sixteen years just under 188,500 saloons and Vans were sold. And, although Isuzu gave up on passenger cars many years ago, the Florian's DNA lives on deep inside today's Isuzu D-Max pick-up.

Above: Reduced specification and prices made the Jaguar 340 a performance bargain.

Opposite: Run-out on the runway: 340 allowed Jaguar to take off into the new XJ6 era.

1967 JAGUAR 340

On 26 September 1967, Jaguar announced the 340 and, with it, the run-out period began for the compact sports saloon that had done so much to swell its Coventry coffers in the 1950s and '60s. The first 'Project Utah' model, the 2.4-litre (retrospectively called the 'Mk1') had arrived in 1956, bringing with it integral monocoque construction. Yet it was the heavily revised Mk2 of 1959 that everyone took pride in, whether as a sign of personal success, a ferocious racing machine or even, sometimes, the perfect getaway car for a bank robbery. Now, with the sensational XJ6 just one year away from launch, the Mk2's rule as the Big Cat's mainstay was coming to a close.

Jaguar decided to carefully adjust the specification and so slash the retail cost of the 340, which replaced the Mk2 3.4-litre, and the 240, which did the same for the Mk2 2.4-litre (the 3.8-litre engine, though was discontinued in advance of the impending 4.2-litre XJ6). They were priced at a keen £1,422 and £1,365 respectively. The last of the 3.4-litres had been listed at £1,764, so the 340 now seemed an astounding bargain; a Jag for the price of a Rover P6. And it remained truly a high-performance car with its 210bhp engine, sometimes capable of 125mph and 0–60mph in a growling 9.6 seconds.

How was this done? Well, naturally in the name of saving more than three hundred quid for the 340, sacrifices were made, and synthetics played their part. The 3.4's gorgeous hand-crafted leather upholstery and door panels were now surfaced in ICI's Ambla plastic, and the floor was covered in a cheaper, tufted carpet.

Externally, standard front fog lights were deleted and replaced with circular air vents, while the double-deck chrome bumpers were changed to thinner, single-profile ones, which looked less clumsy and old-fashioned anyway, and saved a few pounds of excess weight. Tyres remained as cheaper crossplies, although Pirelli Cinturato radials were available at, of course, extra cost, as was power steering.

Faithful to its nature as a stopgap, the 340 was on sale for just one year and discontinued in September 1968. Its sales total of 2,788 cars makes it one of the rarest Jaguar saloons of all time and – but for the lack of luxury – one of the best of the Utahs, and a natural as a 'lost car' for this book. Some police forces, including Hertfordshire, took advantage of the reduced price and bought a few as rapid pursuit and motorway patrol cars, despite their drawbacks of inadequate ventilation, ground clearance and boot space.

As for the poverty-spec 240, that one soldiered on in production until as late as April 1969, using up all the remaining Mk2-type parts inventory. With 4,446 made, it was more commonplace than the 340, but had benefitted even more by its transition from Mk2, its power upped from 120 to 133bhp and its torque improved too, thanks to a straight-port type cylinder head and twin SU HS6 carburettors with a new inlet manifold. So even the least desirable Jaguar of all could now make it to 104mph …

Above: Two-tone paintwork and fancy wheels on the Jeepster Convertible made waves.

Opposite: A preview of SUVs to come: the Jeepster Commando in four-seater station wagon form.

1967 JEEP JEEPSTER 101 COMMANDO

A full five years after the International Scout created the sport-utility genre, Jeep was ready with its response. Yet it was the 1965 arrival of the leisure-tilted Ford Bronco that had really kicked Jeep's butt into action, signalling that the Detroit heavyweights had sized up this niche sector and concluded it had legs. As the global 4×4 pioneer, Jeep should have been in there an awful lot sooner.

Jeepster was a revival of the name given to a much earlier Jeep car, a two-wheel drive open-top 'Sports Phaeton' of 1948 that was ahead of its time as a predictor of American motoring tastes, and therefore had been a failure.

So, better late than never then for Kaiser Jeep Corporation from Toledo, Ohio, and the '67 Jeepster was certainly a striking vehicle on its 101in wheelbase, shared with the mostly for export CJ-6 Universal and giving a much less hoppy ride than the standard CJ-5. It mixed a cocktail of recognisable Jeep features in the separate mudguards, seven-slot grille and high ground clearance with a wider body for a more roomy cockpit.

The Jeepster Commando came in three versions sharing the same basic architecture: a four-seater Roadster with a canvas hood or no roof at all, a two-seater Pick-up, and a four-seater Station Wagon, with the tops bolted-on (and not easy to take off!). They all benefitted from full wind-down windows and door locks, and front bucket seats with pleated vinyl upholstery.

Four-wheel drive was standard across the board, and off-road performance was predictably very capable. Meanwhile, power unit choices split Jeepsters into two camps. For economy there was the 2.2-litre, four-cylinder Hurricane descended directly from the engines in the original wartime Jeeps, and with just 75bhp it could be purchased only with a three-speed manual transmission as it was too underpowered to handle an automatic. No such issue with the other engine, the Dauntless 3.7-litre V6, which could generate a gutsy 160bhp and so additionally came with a General Motors Turbo-Hydramatic three-speed auto.

At the pinnacle of the range was the fanciest version of all: the Jeepster Convertible. Fundamentally the same car as the Commando Roadster, the Convertible came resplendent in a jazzy two-tone colour scheme (white was always one half), split with chrome trim mouldings so the bonnet and decklid were in contrasting colours. Colour-co-ordinated floor mats enlivened the interior, and styled hubcaps with central spinners gave the wheels a lift. The folding roof incorporated a glass rear screen, and at the back was a 'Continental' spare wheel with matching cover.

American Motors acquired Kaiser Jeep in 1969, and after 1971 it didn't use the Jeepster name any more, sticking to just plain Commando, and latterly with a restyled front with four headlights; 57,350 Jeepster 101 Commandos were sold in total, and this included 100 Hurst Special editions loaded with performance and styling extras. One of the advertising slogans for the Jeepster was 'Happy combo – racy and rugged', and that sums it up well. You'd be pretty happy to get hold of a Convertible, or even a Hurst, these days, as they're keenly sought after.

Below: 'You want me to do what?' Stirling Moss and the Fronte SS 360 in Rome in 1968.

Opposite: The tiny Fronte was loved by children and adults in Japan, and was in huge demand.

1967 SUZUKI FRONTE 360

Suzuki's Suzulight 360 of 1962 was a tiny car that, like Britain's Mini, utilised front-wheel drive and a transversely mounted engine, this compact powertrain permitting more passenger space. It seems bewildering that, in 1967, Suzuki would ditch the configuration for an engine at the back, yet the *Kei* car class of city runabouts was a key battleground for Japanese firms to snag first-time buyers, and Subaru's 360 – like a tiny Volkswagen Beetle with its air-cooled power unit in its sloping tail – was the sector's unassailable top-seller. Suzuki decided it must start afresh, with something similar.

The Fronte 360 (code-named LC10) was its answer, and its all-new, two-stroke, 356cc, air-cooled engine was at the back driving the rear wheels. It was a triple-cylinder also equipped with three dinky carburettors, developing 25bhp, and with seven crankshaft bearings to cope with spirited driving through its four-speed manual transmission, with no synchromesh on first gear (that was added in 1969). Top speed was 58mph. Prototypes were thrashed in hot weather in Thailand, and below-zero conditions in Hokkaido, as well as on Suzuki's test track at Ryūyō, to test in particular its all-independent suspension system.

The four seats were inside a cheekily charming saloon car body, and the styling along the waistline was the first on any *Kei* car to adopt the undulating 'Coke bottle' contours then vogueish on American sedans twice the length of the 2.9m Fronte 360. Japanese kids joked that it looked like a Daruma roly-poly doll, and there was much affection for the car from their parents when it was revealed in March 1967, blanket-advertised in a novel TV campaign, and seen in showrooms nationwide on 27 May.

Suzuki intended to make 3,000 Fronte 360s a month at its Kosai assembly plant, but demand was so huge that monthly orders soon rose to 8,000 and would stay there for the whole of the car's life … permanently eclipsing the Subaru 360. An additional factory opened in Iwata in August 1967 to feed the clamour.

The Fronte SS 360 of November 1968 scored a notable innovation in becoming the first high-performance *Kei* car, with a 36bhp engine that could be revved up to a frenzied 7,000pm … and so a rev counter was now included! To launch the car with panache, Suzuki employed Formula 1 legend Stirling Moss and TT-winning Japanese motorbike racer Mitsuo Itoh to drive two SSs along the 466 miles of the Autostada Del Sole from Rome to Naples in a foot-to-the-floor demonstration run. The two maestros averaged 76.08mph – amazing for a car with a 78mph top speed. There was a 475cc export-only version, but neither this nor the SS was sold in Europe. If you didn't see Stirling buzz by that once, then that was it!

A raft of changes followed during 1969, including an all-black interior with revised dashboard, an SS Standard with the hot engine but plain trim, and an S that had the puny engine but the SS's fancy livery. The ultimate boy-racer edition was the lurid SSS of April 1970 before LC10 production concluded six months later.

1967 OSI SILVER FOX

Half-car, half-catamaran, this intriguing machine was intended to demonstrate what could be achieved aerodynamically with a small engine. In the left-hand hull the driver sat ahead of the 1.1-litre Renault-Alpine engine, in the right one the passenger had the spare wheel behind. Between them three wings helped create a super-low 0.258 drag co-efficient.

1967 PININFARINA BMC 1800

Pininfarina's designer Leonardo Fioravanti shaped one of the most influential cars of the 1960s in this wind-cheating interpretation of the UK's Austin-Morris 1800. It was revealed at the 1967 Turin motor show. Unfortunately, other companies, and not BMC, were to pick up on the sleek, 'two-box' look, most notably for the Citroën CX.

Below: The Trident Clipper served up style and V8 power for a lot less than an AC Cobra.

Opposite: It looked just as good from the back – this car had been planned as a future TVR.

1967 TRIDENT CLIPPER

If the original plan had worked out, this handsome grand tourer would have changed the destiny of Blackpool's TVR in the second half of the 1960s. It would have been the go-to British luxury sports car for anyone who couldn't quite afford an E-type or a DB6, and expunged all traces of TVRs as fast but decidedly shed-built two-seaters.

For, in 1964, TVR decided it should be chasing a more affluent, worldly and less DIY clientele, but still with a car offering the shattering performance of its homespun Griffith with its 5-litre V8 engine identical to that in the Shelby Cobra. To make this giant leap, it employed a freelance British stylist, Trevor Fioré (original name: Trevor Frost), who had some useful connections in Italy – then the epicentre of the car design universe.

Fioré designed the car, a really rather beautiful fastback named the TVR Trident, and then negotiated with Turin's Carrozzeria Fissore to construct the first prototype in time for the Geneva motor show in March 1965. They'd hit on a winning formula from the get-go, and TVR was thrilled to be holding £150,000-worth of orders by the time the show closed. Four months later, the firm went bankrupt, unable to persuade its irate creditors of the riches that lay ahead if only they could hold on. Fissore was building two more prototypes, and was not best pleased when payments from Blackpool stopped abruptly.

It was not to be, and in the carve up by liquidators one of TVR's own dealers in Suffolk, William 'Bill' Last, snapped up the Trident design and rights, and decided to make a go of it himself. He had experience in the industry already with the Peel Viking (see p. 90) but the Trident was massively more ambitious and, in fact, styling aside, he almost had to start again from scratch.

The TVR Trident featured TVR's steel spaceframe chassis. Last's Trident Clipper had to have a glass fibre body on an adapted Austin-Healey 3000 frame. The heart of the car remained, though: a 270bhp 5-litre Ford V8 and matching four-speed manual gearbox. The new version was revealed at the Racing Car Show in London in January 1967, conventional headlights replacing futuristic retractable ones, and its £1,923 price temptingly south of the £2,952 AC/Shelby Cobra. Last declared it a 150mph car (never independently verified) and hence fitted huge front disc brakes. Buyers could have their Clippers luxuriously personalised with leather upholstery, shagpile carpets, air conditioning, and even a TV.

Always notionally desirable, the Clipper never quite made it because of the under-capitalisation of the one-man-band Trident company. In 1969 Last launched his Venturer, a cheaper 120mph sister model with a 3.0-litre Ford V6 engine in a Triumph TR6 chassis, while the 1971 Trident Tycoon used the TR6 engine and frame, plus automatic transmission. The fact these two were offered in kit form for home-build – something the original TVR Trident was trying to get right away from – was all part of the company's decline. The Datsun 240Z now did much the same thing but with global backing and quality, so Trident's demise was inevitable, despite those winning looks. In total around eighty cars were made.

Above: Triumph's TR5 was the first British production car with a fuel-injected engine.

Opposite: Minilite magnesium wheels on this one, but the standard car sported Rostyle fake alloys.

1967 TRIUMPH TR5

The popular TR sports-car line was skilfully adapted by Triumph to the more demanding 1960s, and this sixth distinct edition carried an important technical innovation: it was the first production British-built car with a fuel-injected engine, until now confined to expensive German models and bespoke racing machines.

Under the bonnet with its characterful raised-eyebrow headlights was the 2.5-litre power unit, the first six-cylinder engine in a TR and perfected from an experimental engine raced in a Triumph 2000 in the 1966 British Saloon Car Championship. Bored out from the 2.0-litre for extra capacity, the stroke was increased from 76 to 95mm, giving excellent torque but insufficient power for Triumph's high-performance aspirations. So experts were consulted at Lucas Industries and a mechanical fuel-injection system was specified, heavily based on the one used in Jaguar's 1957 Le Mans-winning D-type, and some Maserati road cars. The delivery of pressurised fuel to the cylinders in precisely metered quantities was transformational. Power rose from 104 to 150bhp, giving surging acceleration and plentiful mid-range acceleration to enjoy on the road. The new engine even weighed 3kg (6.6lb) less than the now-obsolete TR4A's 'four' with its old-fashioned carburettors.

The rest of the Michelotti-styled car was similar to the TR4A. The all-synchromesh four-speed gearbox continued, with overdrive a desirable option, and the separate chassis frame was near-identical except for strengthened engine, propshaft and rear axle mountings to handle the 35 per cent torque boost, plus stiffer springs to beef up the suspension.

Inside was a wood dashboard thoughtfully revised with matt finishes to cut out reflections. The hood was easy to fold and very effective at sealing out draughts and rain, and the TR4A's optional hardtop continued with its lift-out roof panel – launched many years ahead of Porsche's 911 Targa roof – and standby 'Surrey' fold-back feature. Eagle-eyed car spotters could identify the new TR5 by its Rostyle imitation-alloy wheel trims, if optional wire wheels weren't fitted, and a 'TR5 PI' boot lid badge.

However, that also identifies the unfortunate issue with this otherwise fine car. The Lucas Mark 2 fuel-injection, and its accuracy of fuel delivery, was originally thought to be helpful in making the TR5 meet emissions laws in the USA, substantially the TR4A's key market. Yet the regulations, especially in the avowedly anti-smog California where TRs sold best, suddenly became much more stringent. To make the TR5 comply would need additional pollution control equipment, whose cost would wipe out any sales profits.

To maintain commercial success required a retrograde step technologically. So the US version was the hastily concocted Triumph TR250, with twin Stromberg carburettors, a much lower state of tune, and power curtailed to 105bhp, almost the same as the TR4A. A chucklesome irony is that the TR250 was given prominent go-faster stripes! It had to be done, though, and the sales figures tell the story. Triumph built just 2,947 TR5s in fourteen months to September 1968 and the debut of the replacement TR6 … but 8,484 TR250s. And it didn't help that the British mechanical fuel injection proved quite unreliable, in galling contrast to Germany's seamless Bosch electronic system …

121

Below: A touch of evening glamour suits the Volvo 142, very popular in northern Europe.

Opposite: The 142 was tough as old boots; this one's a 2.0-litre, superseding the original 1.8.

1967 VOLVO 142

It's hard to suggest a better candidate for practical and comfortable everyday driving than a member of the Volvo 140 series, seen first in August 1966 as the 144. Engineered for life on Scandinavia's harsh roads and freezing conditions, you couldn't find anything more robust. And with global traffic levels intensifying, it marked a major new safety paradigm.

Yes, safety features on this car transformed buyers' expectations, almost overnight, of what every car should encompass. The super-strong steel structure had a built-in roll-over bar in the roof and scientifically shaped, energy-absorbing crumple zones front and rear, with the petrol tank later repositioned to guard against rupture in a crash and side-impact bars installed in the doors. There were disc brakes all round and a failsafe dual-circuit braking system, each one triangulated to rein in three wheels.

Inside, the cabin was shaped with no protruding parts, and three-point front seatbelts were standard – still exceptional then. In 1967 came optional rear seatbelts (three-point ones by 1972), and in 1968 the front seats all had head restraints to mitigate against whiplash in an accident. Volvo's world-first backwards-facing child's seat was also available.

Early 140s used Volvo's 1.8-litre B18 engine, but it was quickly upgraded to the 2.0-litre B20, with a four-speed manual gearbox or, for extra money, overdrive or a three-speed automatic transmission. Volvo made the 140 range simple to comprehend: the second digit in each model's name indicated the number of cylinders (for there was also a six-cylinder 164), and the third one referred to doors: the 142 had two, the 144 four, the 145 estate five. An 'S' suffix meant a sportier twin-carburettor engine, an 'E' broadcast electronic fuel injection. The 140 series was current until 1974, selling 1.2 million cars.

The 142 features here for its rarity, especially in the UK, where it was only offered between 1967 and 1969 and could never be ordered with an automatic gearbox. It proved popular in other parts of northern Europe but didn't really work as an entry-level model. As with the Ford Corsair (see p. 50), two doors was viewed as a negative for practicality. Of the 412,986 142s made, precious few crossed the English Channel.

Yet the 142 was probably the toughest version of all with its additional torsional strength and just four, rather than six, side windows. It became the preferred Volvo for rallying as it was 40kg (88lb) lighter than the equivalent 144, and today is quite sought after as a car for tackling classic events. From a parent's view, too, the longer front doors and tipping front seats led on to a back seat that could accommodate even teenage children without whining about cramped leg- or headroom.

Did the 142 have downsides? A handful. With no power assistance available, the steering was heavy, so relishing the excellent 21ft turning circle required muscles. With the 1.8 engine, or else without an extra carb or fuel injection, performance was leisurely. The cavernous boot has quite a high sill. And that really is about it for criticisms of a very well-built car purpose-designed to protect you.

Below: Hip to be square? The Willam rekindled France's love of the 'microcar'.

Opposite: It's a Willam Farmer, offered briefly in the UK, taking on a thimble-full of fuel.

1967 WILLAM / LAWIL CITY

Petrol-sipping bubble cars had all but faded into motoring history when this bizarre vehicle appeared in prototype form at the 1966 Paris motor show. At a mere 1.78m long, it made a Citroën 2CV seem positively excessive, and under the shortest bonnet in the world lurked a 123cc Lambretta scooter engine, a rowdy two-stroke, single-cylinder that generated all of 5.6bhp to turn the rear wheels. This particular show had seen more than its fair share of follies over its many years, and this ridiculous-looking, two-seater metal box seemed certain to join them.

But no. The person behind it, Henri Willame, was deadly serious. This Lilliputian car was just the thing for growing traffic in France's cities and, what's more, as a 'quadricycle' it could be driven without a full licence and incur a tiny rate of annual road tax. The Willam was on sale by April 1967, and quickly rekindled a French love for micro-motoring that's continued to this day.

The car wasn't actually French, though. M Willame had established Costruzioni Meccaniche e Automobilistiche SpA with designer-entrepreneur Carlo Lavezzari (Lawil combining their names) in Pavia, Lombardy, Italy, to make the vehicles there. Willame was the proprietor of France's Lambretta scooter import company in Paris, and he'd begun to hear rumours that manufacture of the two-wheelers would soon be ending (true as it transpired). So, to keep his business going, he decided to switch into tiny vans and cars that could take advantage of French tax laws, and offer buyers the ultimate in thrift.

Lambretta's own three-wheeled van, the 1960–65 Lambro FLi series, had already blazed a trail for him. Indeed, the Lawil partners engaged Italian firm Scattolini to assemble the Willam City, as it had formerly supplied metal pressings to Lambretta for the discontinued Lambro and still exists today making commercial vehicle bodies. Important to note, however, that although there were many Lambretta connections, the scootering legend wasn't part of this project.

The four-speed gearbox could be 'inverted' to give the same four speeds backwards, while a larger 175cc engine option did require its master to have a driving licence, but this proved unpopular and was canned in 1970. By then the standard car had been stretched to 2.05m long to add some cargo space. By far the most successful Willam, however, was a rather pleasing 60cm-longer van that would prove enduringly popular because, pluckily, it could handle a 400kg (882lb) load.

In 1971, Italian sales started as the Lawil Varzina. It was the country's smallest domestically made motor car, with a 246cc Lambretta twin-cylinder engine upgrade and 10in rather than 8in wheels, and a conventional four-speed-plus-reverse transmission. With 12bhp of power, a startling 40mph was now feasible, 5–10mph more than with the 125. An open two-seater with a plastic body called the Farmer was introduced too, with 'safety' chains in place of doors; a small number of these were later sold in the UK by Crayford Auto Developments of Westerham, Kent. Everything bar the van was dropped in 1980, but Willam marketed a bewildering number of other tiny Italian-made road-going contraptions until his business closed down in 1988.

1968 FORD CAPRI PROTOTYPE

It's well-known that the Capri was conceived as Europe's own Ford Mustang, a sporty (not out-and-out sports) car that could be tailored to each individual customer. Less well-known is that the Capri's distinctive semicircular rear side windows were a very last-minute change, as this close-to-finalised prototype undergoing cold weather testing clearly shows.

1968 BERTONE ALFA ROMEO CARABO

At an exceptionally fertile time for car design, Bertone still managed to shock and awe with this Alfa Romeo 33 racer-based, wedge-shaped supercar, the work of Marcello Gandini. It was significant for its world-first adoption of 'scissor doors', and the Carabo proved a major inspiration for the 1971 Lamborghini Countach that had those too.

Above: American Motors' answer to the Ford Mustang; check out the styled front bumper.

Opposite: The Javelin came only as this fastback coupé but with a wide range of options.

1968 AMC JAVELIN

American Motors Corporation was the last of the four big North American manufacturers with a 'pony car', US vernacular for the Ford Mustang and its imitators. Its slick and eye-catching styling was a notable achievement for AMC, and the compact (by US standards) hardtop Javelin proved remarkably popular for a total newcomer. At least to begin with.

The Javelin was half of AMC's twin-pronged effort to overturn its dowdy image, developed alongside the short-wheelbase AMX coupé, which became well liked among horsepower addicts for its hearty showing in US track racing and hot-rodding – and for being the country's only other two-seater production car besides the Chevrolet Corvette.

Mechanical hardware was drawn from AMC's Rambler American sedans, including conventional coil springs/wishbones front suspension, with semi-elliptic leaf springs at the back. Around this, California-born chief stylist Richard Teague created his arrestingly uncluttered fastback shape, with a so-called 'twin-venturi' radiator grille mounted quite high up with a deep, wraparound styled apron chrome bumper below. Teague was a classic car fanatic, a one-time design chief at Packard, and since 1960 had worked wonders for AMC with slender resources and constant management turmoil. The Javelin was among his best work.

A wide array of options and styling packages was on the showroom menu, and the sporty SST was among the most popular. Engines ranged from a 3.8-litre straight-six, not hugely powerful but giving 24mpg, up to V8s of 4.6-, 5.6- and even 6.4-litre capacity with power ranging from 225 to 315bhp. Even the six could be specified with beefed-up suspension and anti-roll bar; meanwhile, a 6.4 V8 Javelin with the full 'Go' pack including front disc brakes and super-wide tyres had furious 0–60mph acceleration of seven seconds and a hefty 426lb ft of torque. These four-seater cars were lighter than close competitor ponies, giving them a definite performance edge.

Safety and style had been intertwined with flush-fitting door handles and, inside, a moulded-plastic, one-piece dashboard with spongy padding that extended up the screen pillars. All Javelins had individual front bucket seats, despite the steering column gear shifter, but there were never any convertibles, unlike for rival Mustangs and Firebirds – AMC didn't have the capital required to tool up for them.

The firm did allocate budget to take its Javelin racing, though, and the factory-backed team made a plucky showing in Sports Car Club of America Trans-Am racing in 1968. Overall success eluded it until 1970 when the Penske Racing Team took on the management task for AMC, with its star driver Mark Donohue, who managed to bag overall second place in the season championship for the Javelin. The kudos was well deserved, and there was a sell-out edition of 2501 Mark Donohue Special Javelin SSTs with a big rear spoiler. Sales-wise, the Javelin shifted an impressive 70,000 cars in 1968, but in that buoyant pony car era tastes were fickle, and 1969 sales were down to 40,000, and 30,000 in 1970. The Javelin had a total restyle for 1971 as AMC tried to morph it from pony car to muscle car but never quite hit the sporty car target again.

Above: The Corcel sold poorly until this two-door coupé version shook off the taxi image.

Opposite: The Renault 12 lineage is easy to spot in the centre part of the Corcel four-door saloon.

1968 FORD CORCEL

Mention of the Renault Dauphine built under licence by Willys Overland do Brasil on p. 30 reminds us this rear-engined family car was a pillar of the Brazilian motor industry. With international finance and local shareholders, well-resourced Willys could make everything required for this and its locally built Jeeps, and 75,000 Dauphines were sold. In 1965, Willys and Renault envisaged a bigger, more modern stablemate, Renault's critical new front-wheel drive saloon code-named Project M.

Car ownership was now a reasonable ambition for the Brazilian middle classes – there were 'consumers' to satisfy, and a developing road network to exploit. So Willys Overland engineer Marcos Mello departed for France and spent a year there actively involved in planning Project M, putting the case for the specific ruggedness and simplicity his country demanded. Seven prototypes attuned for Brazilian motoring were built and assessed.

Renault must have been livid when, in 1967, Ford boldly grabbed a controlling stake in Willys Overland do Brasil. The intellectual property of its important new product had been freely shared; now an aggressive multinational rival was getting access to it. Ford apparently even sneaked a prototype back to Detroit to extract its secrets. It must have been doubly galling to see the Brazilian version fast-tracked to the market on 26 September 1968 as the Ford Corcel … a year before the French could unveil their own as the Renault 12!

True, the Corcel featured a bigger boot, opening front door quarterlights, and circular headlamps, but essentially they were one and the same. Ford could maybe have produced its European Escort in Brazil, but thanks to Renault the Corcel was ready to roll. The 1.3-litre, in-line, four-cylinder engine produced a meek 68bhp to give an 80mph top speed, and transmission was an all-synchromesh four-speed manual. The entire independent coil-spring suspension system with anti-roll bars front and back was near identical to the Renault 12's, as were the three-nut fastenings on the wheels, and front disc brakes.

The Corcel's early hiccups no doubt induced a delightful sensation of *schadenfreude* in Paris. Private buyers stubbornly resisted the four-door saloon, feeling it was too taxi-like, and when a coupé edition was launched in August 1969, strongly redolent of a small Ford Mustang, it quickly became the better seller. There would never be a Renault 12 equivalent of that one.

The 12 enjoyed a blameless reputation in Europe. Not, though, the Corcel in South America. Poor build quality and steering alignment gave it a patchy reputation from day one. This compelled Ford, facing a customer rout and now under fierce competition in Brazil from Volkswagen and General Motors, to chalk up an unfortunate innovation: the first customer recall in Brazilian car-making history. Owners were asked politely to take their cars – including a new two-door estate, the Belina – to local dealers to have the steering fixed.

Ford's ownership of the issue meant the Corcel's reputation was mostly salvaged. The first generation continued until 1977, when an outwardly brand-new range appeared. Yet underneath everything was still exactly as for the Renault 12; the 2,440mm wheelbase was identical, as were those three-nut-hole wheels!

Above: The Islero was subtle, fast and exclusive – one of Ferruccio Lamborghini's favourites.

Opposite: Tiny bumpers above the rear lights to ward off car park dents …

1968 LAMBORGHINI ISLERO

There is much mystique to Lamborghini in the 1960s; the revenge on an arrogant Enzo Ferrari and, of course, the birth of the exotic supercar in the sensational, mid-engined Lamborghini Miura. What's sometimes overlooked, as he was more an enabler than a car designer, is the essentially humble and pragmatic nature of Ferruccio Lamborghini himself. His prosperity came from agriculture, tractors and heating boilers, and the GT car he originally backed was a powerful, luxurious and handsome statement of success for hard workers just like him.

So while his car company made outlandish design statements in the Miura and four-seater Espada, the boss's heart remained in the urbane continental express the earliest 350GT and 400GT represented. The little-known Islero became their direct, and spiritual, successor for a select and particular group of buyers.

Where Miura was named after a famous Spanish bullfighter, Islero was a bull that had gored his matador opponent in a 1947 battle. The fast-beating heart of this beast was Lamborghini's quadruple-camshaft 4.0-litre V12 engine with no fewer than six Weber 40 DCOE carburettors, mounted in a shorter (than the 400GT) tubular-framed chassis with all-round independent suspension. Lamborghini's own five-speed manual gearbox even had synchromesh on reverse. Unlike on the Miura, the longitudinally mounted engine up front called for a long bonnet, behind which was the intimate two-plus-two accommodation. This car was for blasting across Europe on sweeping highways on its gorgeous Campagnolo magnesium wheels, costly to fuel and maintain, and much rarer to encounter than Ferrari or Maserati equivalents.

Ferruccio's original GTs carried elegant bodies designed by Carrozzeria Touring, which was defunct by 1966. One of its key former employees, Carlo Marazzi, had since established his own coachworks with his son Mario, and Lamborghini contracted them to design (with Ferruccio's attentive guidance) and make the Islero coachwork, which because of Marazzi's stretched resources did result in a few minor teething problems. The Islero's overall profile followed the 400GT's, giving a rakish and immaculate image enhanced by adding four headlights in retractable pods. Sumptuous leather upholstery and a fully stocked dashboard, meanwhile, made it every inch the Italian thoroughbred for the discerning, self-made millionaire. The car was revealed at the Geneva motor show in March 1968. Ferruccio Lamborghini, naturally, drove one daily, as did his brother Edmondo.

For many people, the Espada was much more exciting, and the two cars made Lamborghini unusual in offering a contrasting choice of V12 luxury GTs into which young children (or short friends) could squeeze. The original 325bhp Islero was capable of 155mph. After 155 of those had been sold it was updated to Islero S specification, ventilation improved and windows tinted, with 350bhp meaning it could top 160mph; only another seventy of these were made before, in 1969, the Islero was discontinued, and Lamborghini expanded into smaller, V8-engined models like the Urraco, plus its later Countach supercar. It was both an obscure and an obsolete machine when an Islero took a prominent role in the 1970 Roger Moore movie thriller *The Man Who Haunted Himself*, one of the five right-hand drive examples produced.

Above: LMX Sirex was plastic-bodied, unlike other coach-built Italian sports cars.

Opposite: Dependable Ford components were used throughout, including a Taunus V6 engine.

1968 LMX SIREX

This elusive two-seater sports car is of the type common to the UK during the 1960s and early '70s because of its harnessing of someone else's engine in a plastic body. The Sirex is an anomaly for Italy, though. With a sounder financial footing the venture might have been a success, but Alfa Romeo, Fiat and Lancia had the sports car market sewn up anyway. Over five frustrating years no more than fifty were delivered.

The most noteworthy aspect of the car was its miniature Corvette styling from the pen of ex-Bertone genius Franco Scaglione. His Alfa Romeo 33 Stradale is often acclaimed as the most beautiful interpretation of the mid-engined GT coupé, and his canon of esteemed work stretched back to the early 1950s. In his freelance later period he was hired by two entrepreneur partners in LMX Automobile Srl of Turin to give their car credibility. It stood for Linea Moderna Executive. Frenchman Michele Liprandi and Italian Giovanni Mandelli ran a workshop called Limaplas, moulding glass fibre bodies for Abarth and De Tomaso racing cars, and now wanted to do their own thing. Racecar constructor Gioacchino Colombo designed the chassis with a forked central backbone similar to Britain's Lotus Elan.

Scaglione's body would, naturally, be made of plastic (with steel doors), and for the mechanical parts the team turned to Ford, as presumably no Italian firm wanted to assist a potential rival. LMX chose a 2.3-litre V6 engine from the German Ford Taunus, plus Ford Taunus-derived front suspension and the back axle from the British Zodiac MkIV. Small-scale manufacturers have long been grateful for Ford, which has happily sold parts to anyone, viewing it as useful extra business with no serious threat involved.

The car looked terrific and, with 126bhp in a lightweight coupé, promised a great drive. Yet a whiff of the troubles lying ahead surrounded the very launch at the 1968 Turin motor show where, because LMX couldn't afford a stand (or was it, maybe, denied space after the Italian motor industry 'elite' conspired against it?), the unveiling took place outside the exhibition centre …

Carrozzeria Eurostyle of Turin was appointed contractor to assemble the cars, and wealthy buyers were tempted with options like air conditioning and a (then extremely modern) radio-cassette player. A 210bhp supercharged engine could be ordered too. Admirers, though, were reluctant to step forward as actual customers, and there was barely enough money to pay for the crates of Ford components, never mind fund any marketing. Reviews did not, in general, identify much of the magic that carried the Lotus Elan above its flaws for its outstanding roadholding and ride quality. The Sirex was, predictably, rough round the edges.

By 1973 it was sadly all over. The final twenty cars were built up after closure, and sold in Switzerland. These included one of just two convertibles. Perhaps this version, with the right engine, could have succeeded in the US market, where Alfa Romeo and Fiat 124 Spiders sold most strongly. A single car was delivered to the UK, and last seen in the 1980s.

1968 ITALDESIGN BIZZARRINI MANTA

Several cars in this book owe their distinctive character to Giorgetto Giugiaro, who worked for Ghia and then Bertone. When he set up his independent Italdesign bureau in 1968, this is the concept supercar that launched him as an in-demand freelance. Being based on the Bizzarrini P538 rear-engined racecar meant it had a Chevrolet V8 engine.

1968 VOLVO P1800 PROTOTYPE THE ROCKET

In the late 1960s Volvo started to consider updating its popular P1800 coupé, and decided a sports estate reworking was the way to go. Two imaginative treatments were sought from Italian designers, and the one from Sergio Coggiola eventually became the 1800ES. This was Pietro Frua's interpretation, with its truncated tail imparting a strange and futuristic appearance …

Left: A Grand Prix with the enigmatic Frixos Demetriou. (*Car* magazine)

Opposite: Lombardi's cute little coupé came in many forms, this being the Abarth Scorpione 1300.

1968 LOMBARDI 850 GRAND PRIX

Carlo Francesco 'Francis' Lombardi was a daredevil First World War fighter pilot and then a constructor of trainer aircraft for the next global conflict; an unlikely maker of the diminutive pocket-sized supercar you'll discover here.

In 1947, with Italy's aeronautical industry downed in the Allied defeat of Mussolini, Francis Lombardi needed something else to do. So he started a car coachbuilding company in Vercelli, producing four-door and estate-car versions of various Fiats and Lancias, and some stretched limos, one of which was used by the Pope. Where the impetus arose to build his own sports car is unclear – possibly from in-house designer Giuseppe Rinaldi – but the Grand Prix caused a stir at the 1968 Geneva motor show. This was not only for its wedge-like shape, gamine size and 42in height but also its exotic car details such as pop-up headlamps, large single windscreen wiper, aerodynamic-looking cut-off tail, and an instrument pod in the centre of the dashboard like something from – surprise, surprise – an aeroplane cockpit.

It looked like it was doing 100mph just standing still. In fact, performance was spritely at best, as a completely ordinary Fiat 850 floorpan was used, the rear-mounted 843cc engine cranking out just 37bhp, plus the standard-issue four-speed gearbox.

The first series had a plain, body-colour glass fibre engine cover, but the second generation featured a black-painted one with extra louvres, to denote the hotter 47bhp Fiat 850 Special engine below. Weighing just 630kg (1,389lb) and with tiny doors, it felt anything but slothful, with plenty of engine noise for extra kicks, and really could indeed lick 100mph.

There was more performance to come after the car caught the eye of renowned tuner Carlo Abarth. In autumn 1968 he launched his 52bhp Abarth Grand Prix with the 903cc engine from the Fiat 850 Sport, and a front-mounted radiator to keep it cool. That was the prelude to his ultimate iteration, the 1970 Abarth Scorpione SS with 75bhp, courtesy of a bored-out version of the Fiat 124's 1.2-litre engine, and a specially made bellhousing to marry it to the 850's transmission. With negligible extra weight, this one could hit 110mph, and came with all-round disc brakes and anti-roll bars. Yet another tuning firm, Rome's Giannini Automobili, offered its own 1.0-litre twin-camshaft engine in the car as the Giannini 1000 Grand Prix, as well as working on the OTAS Grand Prix 820, a reduced-capacity edition adapted to US and Canadian laws.

Carlo sold his company and racing team to Fiat in 1971. The first thing Fiat did, with its mid-engined X1/9 imminent, was cancel the Grand Prix and Scorpione, and Francis Lambardi didn't make any more after 1972. It's thought roughly 500 of all types were produced, with ten brought to the UK by Lombardi's British concessionaire Frixos Demetriou, a Cypriot London casino owner briefly and controversially involved in 1969 in importing Italian cars. He was pictured with a grim expression on the cover of January 1969's *Car* magazine alongside the £1,426 right-hand drive Grand Prix. Some of the cars were shipped on to Cyprus, where Mr Demetriou was mysteriously crushed to death in his car one day by an errant army tank.

Above: Un-Familia? The R100 is largely forgotten as the first mass-market rotary-engined car.

Opposite: Coupé body style and circular rear lights denote Mazda's Wankel-engined pioneer.

1968 MAZDA R100

This was Mazda's first rotary-engined production car for the mass market, which makes it the first of all. The pioneering NSU Wankel Spider (see p. 54) and Mazda's 110S Cosmo were esoteric, two-seater sports cars; the R100 was for the everyday motorist, and it gets little credit for spreading the rotary love. Although cramped inside compared to a Ford Escort, the R100 had wolfish performance to startle a 2-litre Capri owner.

First, the engine. Essentially it's the Cosmo unit detuned by 10bhp to 100bhp and with various changes to cheapen costs for mass production, such as cast iron end plates for the rotor housings instead of aluminium. Each of the twin rotor chambers had a 491cc capacity, making this a 982cc car but with equivalence to a 1,964cc reciprocating engine. Hence there was terrific acceleration, because the R100 could, as *Motor* magazine discovered in its January 1970 report, reach 60mph from standstill in a blinding (for the era) 10.9 seconds, and achieve a 108mph top speed. Mazda took it racing at the Spa-Francorchamps 24 Hours endurance race in 1969 and 1970, and both times it finished fifth, harrying factory-backed Porsche 911s.

The rest of the car. The fastback bodywork was a coupé version, exclusive to the R100 and with a unique grille and circular tail lights, of the Familia, Mazda's small family car. Both these rear-wheel drive models took their bow at the 1967 Tokyo motor show, although it was another year before you could purchase an R100, and a year more before exports reached Australia, the UK and the USA (the first Mazda sold in the States).

The uncanny aspect to it was summed up by *Motor*: 'You never realise just how rough and noisy a conventional engine can be until you drive an ordinary four-cylinder car after the Mazda.' The car was so smooth and refined that the engine had to have an electrical device – with an alarm buzzer – to shut down the chokes from the carburettor, so the rotors didn't wear away at more than 6,800rpm under zealous acceleration.

The R100 had Familia-related downsides. Its handling didn't match its eagerness. The front MacPherson struts and leaf-sprung rear axle made it hoppy, not helped by feeble Japanese shock absorbers and skinny, shallow-tread tyres; nevertheless, export cars did have front disc brakes. Front seats were uncomfortable and passenger space in the back tight, although the floor pedal to tip the front seats forward was novel.

The R100 had a bugbear all its own, though. Even for a rapid 2-litre-esque performance car, it guzzled petrol, it was hard to get more than 23mpg overall from it; 18mph was more likely. Poor economy, of course, went on to decimate Mazda rotary sales in the 1970s' fuel crises, but by then it was deeply committed to rotaries in the RX-2, the car for which this one paved the way. The R100 was quietly discontinued in 1973 after 95,706 had been sold. So the R100 took the company in a direction that nearly ruined it; no wonder Mazda doesn't refer to it very often.

Below: The 4 Plein Air is all a big game to some people, but Renault took it seriously.

Opposite: A beach car for the beautiful barefoot people grew out of an experimental battlefield runabout.

1968 RENAULT 4 PLEIN AIR

Evidence that the major French carmakers watched each other like jealous hawks in the 1960s isn't much plainer than this. When Renault announced on 15 May 1968 customers could now order a Plein Air beach car at any dealer, it was twenty-four hours before the plastic-bodied Citroën Mehari competitor was unveiled. A petty spoiler indeed, but then rivalry was fierce. However, as the ill-starred Mini Moke demonstrated in 1968 when British manufacture ended, the market for such a vehicle proved tricky to establish.

And, like the Moke, the Plein Air – meaning Open Air – grew from ambitions to clinch a lucrative military contract. The French Navy had collaborated with specialist commercial vehicle company Sinpar on an open-topped battlefield runabout called the 4×4 Torpedo back in 1964, adapting the front-wheel drive Renault 4 into a go-anywhere 'jeep', aerially deployable by parachute. This mirrored the original Moke project between British armed forces and BMC, and likewise didn't progress far, although French Commando Marines did undertake manoeuvres with ten experimental Torpedos.

Keen to thwart Citroën's Mehari, Renault now commissioned Sinpar to make a simpler, front-drive-only version at its Colombes workshops near Paris, for sale to the beautiful people of the late 1960s who owned villas near a beach, and could use it to drive there in bikinis and trunks – a world away from paratroopers dropping into enemy territory! Part-finished Renault 4 saloons were delivered to Colombes, where Sinpar sawed the roof off and built up new side panels with open cut-outs by way of doors, the inner sills heavily reinforced to keep the car rigid. A Moroccan-market Renault 4 gearbox sump guard was fitted, and a rear anti-roll bar from a Renault 4 van, best to rein in the alarming cornering lean that the torsion bar suspension, soft and forgiving, would lend the much lightened car.

The Plein Air came in white with black side decals, with a crude hanging chain across each door aperture for rudimentary side protection, while the modified windscreen provided an attaching point for a basic plastic soft-top. The 845cc, water-cooled, four-cylinder engine remained unaltered from the regular Renault 4, its characteristic push/pull gear change still sprouting from the dashboard.

One hundred Plein Airs were allocated by Renault for PR duties, with a batch of six right-hand drive Plein Airs ordered by Renault UK for nationwide dealer promotions and special events; these were all repainted yellow in 1970. None was sold new to a customer despite a quoted list price of £815 (costlier than a Ford Cortina MkII), although one survives and has been lovingly restored. In France the hefty list price of 8,990 Francs was a drag on sales, and was more than for the Mehari. It was hardly a beach buggy in the Californian style, while the Mehari found many rural customers who valued its greater versatility and rust-free robustness. Sinpar converted 506 Renault 4s into Plein Airs before it was dropped in March 1970, and replaced by the Renault 4 ACL Rodeo, which, like the Mehari, had plastic bodywork. Interestingly, with 60,000 sold, that one was quite successful, although paltry compared to the 145,000 Meharis built.

Above: Seen as a grown-up Beetle by many, the ugly oval headlights were soon ditched.

Opposite: A 411 in fire chief's car livery, ready for any emergency …

1968 VOLKSWAGEN 411

With the phenomenal popularity of its Beetle across the USA, Volkswagen had every confidence in its rear-mounted, air-cooled engine philosophy, so when it started work on Project EA 142 in 1962 – aka Type 4 as the fourth VW after the original Beetle, Type 2 Transporter van and Type 3 1500/1600 – the strategy seemed foolproof. This was going to be a big family car different to other Volkswagens in just one respect: the first with a full monocoque structure and no separate chassis platform. That stride forward alone was all it needed, the company thought, to grow its appeal. It didn't quite turn out that way.

Unveiled in September 1968 at the Berlin Industrial Fair, the 411 was trumpeted as 'Der Große aus Wolfsburg' (the Big One from Wolfsburg). It was indeed the first VW with four doors on a much longer wheelbase than the Beetle, and newly created four-cylinder, 1.7-litre 'boxer' engine in its fastback tail. The double-jointed, swing-axle rear suspension was similar to the Porsche 911's, while up front was a brand-new MacPherson strut independent set-up.

Buyers could pick from two- or four-door saloons, in standard or L trim, the latter with carpets and velour upholstery. Key 411 pluses included draught-free air circulation, thermostat-controlled auxiliary heating, and six-way, adjustable, fully reclining front seats. Taking a note from Volvo's book, VW emphasised safety with the 411's front and rear crumple zones, padded dashboard and steering wheel, and collapsible steering column. Radial tyres and a three-phase alternator were standard too. The boot was, of course, in the nose of the 411, and could swallow up to 670 litres.

With a modest 68bhp, and despite twin carburettors, the car wasn't that powerful for its size. It was also noisy, like all Volkswagens. Top speed was an unimpressive 90mph, less with the optional automatic transmission. There was little doubting the quality, and the interior was spacious and comfy, but people disliked the early oval headlamps that imbued a slightly deranged frontal appearance, and they were soon changed to two pairs of round ones.

The following year in August came the 80bhp 411 E with electronic Bosch fuel injection, also offered as a three-door 411 E Variant estate car with the engine below the cargo space floor and a fold-down back seat, and air con became an option.

Punchy sales forecasts stressed the need to make 1,000 cars daily. Yet the 411 appealed primarily to existing VW customers, or at least any who actually sought a bigger car, and there simply weren't enough of those. Only one in five transferred allegiance from another marque. In June 1972 the big car became the 412 with assorted small changes, and stayed in production until July 1974, when the new, front-engined, front-wheel drive and water-cooled Passat (derived from the Audi 80) took over. Of the 367,728 VW Type 4s produced, 241,358 were 411s. Possibly as few as 500 are still extant. It's been memorably called a 'respectable flop' for VW, and in the end it wasn't at all a bad car, with all the qualities that drove the Volkswagen Beetle's global impact; just lacking its rebellious charms.

1969 LANCIA FULVIA BARCHETTA

There was never an open version of the desirable Lancia Fulvia HF … except for this racecar, three of which were produced by Cesare Fiorio and Claudio Maglioli to combat the issue of cockpit heat on frenzied international endurance events. The car was 200kg (440lb) lighter too, so they went like the clappers in the 1969 Targa Florio and Tour de Corse. (Autosport)

1969 HOLDEN HURRICANE

This two-seater concept was built by Holden in Australia and restored by the company to a magnificent condition in 2011. With its V8 engine positioned in the middle, it was termed a 'research vehicle' and was packed with electronic devices, such as digital instruments, a wide-angle rear-view CCTV camera, and 'Comfortron' air conditioning.

Above: Adventurous French drivers were asked to try the novel M35 … with full back-up.

Opposite: The coupé body was unique to the Ami-based M35, as was the single-rotor engine.

1969 CITROËN M35

Citroën's hunger for advanced technology inevitably drew it to the rotary engine. A dozen car companies bought licences for Dr Felix Wankel's patented design through his partner NSU, although few committed quite like Citroën. Boss Pierre Bercot convinced his colleagues that rotaries were the single best way forward for the 1970s, and established a joint venture with NSU called Comotor in 1967. It built a factory in Saarlouis, Germany, near the Luxembourg border, where twenty-five rotary power units would be machined daily, rising to 500 a day once sales were humming. Heady stuff.

Part of the groundwork for this expected bonanza was preparing customers to switch over from conventional piston engines. That's where the M35 stepped in. A limited run was planned of 500 working prototypes for sale to selected members of the French public, on condition they'd cover at least 19,000 miles a year and help harvest real-life feedback in this colossal experiment. The 14,120 Franc price (similar to a regular Citroën D Special) included a two-year warranty and a guaranteed loan car, with dedicated telephone rescue hotline, should an M35 conk out.

Citroën created a remarkably bespoke car for the trials. Although the M35 was based on the Ami 8, all the rear coupé body, doors, and even the windscreen were unique, and manufactured by French coachbuilder Heuliez for assembly at Citroën's Rennes plant. Every one sported a rear window sticker that, translated, read: 'This Citroën M35 prototype, fitted with a rotary engine, is undergoing long-term testing at the hands of a Citroën customer.' The reclining, ribbed vinyl seats were like those in the luxury SM. M35 suspension was a floaty DS-style hydropneumatic system, the smallest Citroën ever so equipped.

Its heart was the single-rotor engine, the 497.5cc capacity equivalent to 995cc, allied to a brand-new, four-speed, manual gearbox. With 49bhp available, it would never be fast, although nor was it slouchy, and the forgiving ride quality was exceptional for such a small vehicle. Zero–60mph took nineteen seconds, much livelier than an Ami 8. Once turning above 3,000rpm, the whirring power unit was super smooth. Through the single-spoke steering wheel the driver had to monitor the standard rev counter because 7,000rpm was all the engine could take.

On one level, the M35 succeeded. It led directly to the GS Birotor of 1973, with a twin-rotor engine, which briefly enjoyed full production car status before being abruptly abandoned during an acute fuel crisis (like all rotaries, petrol consumption was excessive), and Citroën's own insolvency. And the M35's suspension and gearbox were later used in all GSs.

On another level, it failed. Citroën only made 267 of the planned 500; each car was numbered externally but there was a gap between No. 175 and No. 376 that the company calculated no one would notice – France is a big country, after all. Many M35 engines malfunctioned before reaching 40,000 miles, and in 1971 Citroën offered a generous trade-in deal to take them back, and destroy them. Anybody who kept one had to sign Citroën's agreement that any obligation to stock spare parts for them was lifted, and 100 brave owners did. There are thought to be sixty left.

Above: The Dacia 1300 was identical in almost all respects to France's 1969 Renault 12.

Opposite: The Dacia 1300 estate with, behind it, a Dacia 1100, the Romanian-assembled Renault 8.

1969 DACIA 1300

After the Ford Corcel (see p. 130) the Renault 12 yet again has a disguised role in this book as the basis of the Dacia 1300. Incredibly, this Romanian beauty also, like the Corcel, stole the 12's thunder by sneakily making its debut before the original design, in this case nine days before, when the Dacia was a star attraction in Romania's annual August Parade on 23 August 1969.

Several years in planning, the Dacia was a big deal. Under the Communist regime of Nicolae Ceaușescu rapid industrialisation was in full swing, intended to bring national self-sufficiency to the Balkan country. Romania had no car industry as yet and therefore needed a partner, and found one in Renault. Plans were shared for its new 12, a state-of-the-art four-door family car with front-wheel drive. Dacia, however, urgently needed car-making experience, and so took on an initial licence to assemble the outdated, rear-engined Renault 8 from imported kits, at its Mioveni plant, selling it as the Dacia 1100 from 1968.

The 1300, with its 1.3-litre four-cylinder engine mounted longitudinally, made good sense. It was spacious, sure-footed, functional and cheap to run, just like the 12. It was safe and comfortable. Any questions of whether the car was humdrum or not were irrelevant; for most Romanians the 1300 was the first car they'd ever drive, and the only one they could hope to buy in that closed-off, forbidding totalitarian state, with its evil dictator and his wife Elena in iron-grip charge. No wonder early exports for the Dacia 1300 are said to have included North Korea.

Renault's terms in those early days restricted the Dacia 1300 from entering markets where the 12 was on sale. Although hard evidence cannot be corroborated, it seems likely build integrity was not quite up to western European standards anyway; the 1300 was of mediocre quality, and its body quite corrosion prone. Then again, the 12 itself was no angel in that respect. In 1970, Dacia presented its 1301 version, with a more inviting interior likely to please government officials, and in 1973 came the 1300 Break five-door estate car. In 1975, Dacia added the 1302 pick-up truck, and extremely popular it was too. By the mid-1980s self-sufficiency was reached when 98.5 per cent of the manufactured car represented entirely local content.

Before very long it was so outdated as to be positively unsafe, front disc brakes notwithstanding, yet descendants of the 1300 were still available in 2004, and the pick-up lasted until 2006. Some 2 million examples were sold. They seemed massively behind the times by then, with no airbags, anti-lock brakes or air conditioning ever offered. Survivors from before the 1979 arrival of the mildly updated 1310, due to the forementioned rust, are rarely encountered on its home territory. Romania's 'people's car' comfortably outlived Nicolae and Elena Ceaușescu, who were both shot by firing squad in 1989 when their terrifying reign ended in a revolution that heralded democracy and freedom. Unlike East Germany's iconic Trabant, though, the western media was not flooded with TV images of Dacia 1300s joyously mobbing the border …

Above: The rare and highly desirable R130 Luce was only sold to wealthy Japanese customers.

Opposite: Styling for this refined and relaxed cruiser was by Giugiaro when he worked at Bertone.

1969 MAZDA R130 LUCE

It's 1969 and 'peak rotary', with the silken new engine technology poised to change the automobile forever. Companies everywhere had taken out manufacturing licences from NSU for Dr Wankel's design; prototypes were hurtling around test tracks, buyers were getting excited. Goodbye pistons – here comes the future.

It fell to Mazda to bravely market rotary-powered offerings to the mass car market, beginning with the R100 (see p. 140), and throughout the early 1970s it added rotary versions to all its model ranges. That extended even to utility vehicles like pick-ups and minibuses.

The company originally developed the 110S Cosmo in 1963 as a futuristic 'halo' car and rotary showcase. Now, ironically, appearing rather dated, it was time for something new and in 1967 the company revealed its RX-87 design concept in Tokyo. The superbly swish two-door hardtop lines came straight from the studio of Giorgetto Giugiaro – lately the lead designer at Italy's Bertone coachbuilding company, and still in his twenties. Superficially, it resembled a sporty version of the Mazda Luce 1500/1800 saloon also styled by Giugiaro-era Bertone.

Under that gracefully tapering bonnet was a specially created twin-rotor 13A in which each chamber had 655cc of capacity, making it nominally a 1310cc power unit yet giving the performance of a conventional one twice as big. The ultra-compact engine was mounted ahead of the front axle line for optimum weight distribution and cabin space, and was only ever used in this single model. Mazda's 'Mr Rotary', Kenichi Yamamoto, tuned 13A for torque rather than outright power, of which it had 126lb ft at a relaxed 3,500rpm (with the rotors spinning almost twice as fast, max power output was 126bhp).

Mazda, though, must have been enviously eyeing the sensational NSU Ro80 because, like that car, the R130 had front-wheel drive – the only rotary-powered Mazda ever with that layout. The Luce R130 went on sale in October 1969, with displays in Japan's leading department stores. It was barely changed from the RX-87 show car, its pillarless style aided by four retractable electric windows, its interior lavishly trimmed and finished. Air conditioning, tweed upholstery, wood-rim steering wheel, rear ashtrays and an eight-track music system were standard equipment.

It was a glamorous, 118mph flagship intended only for unruffled cruising around its home country (it wasn't sold outside Japan) – very expensive and partly hand-built. Yet by October 1972, the order book closed, and the exclusive R130 was over. A mere 976 examples had been delivered. Mazda was now too preoccupied with mainstream rotary models to need this distraction. However, within two years its entire Wankel programme unravelled after an acute global fuel crisis made these always fuel-hungry cars difficult to sell.

One additional factor ushered the R130 into history. Mazda's dalliance with Italian designers ended when it focused on the US export market, and started to design cars in-house that copied the prevailing design trends from the Detroit majors. That meant chunky, often clumsy shapes, finicky details and huge bumpers. It was many years before Mazda made a car as svelte as the rarefied R130 again.

Above: The racy 850 Sport is still, after more than seventy years, Seat's only convertible.

Opposite: The two-seater roadster is a carbon copy of Fiat's own 850 Spider.

1969 SEAT 850 SPORT

Only one soft-top has ever been built by Seat, and this is it. It went on sale the same year the Spanish firm produced its one-millionth car, and was decidedly frivolous next to the staid saloons and estates usually found in Seat showrooms.

Everything the company made since setting up shop outside Barcelona in 1953 had Fiat origins as part of a long-standing collaboration. Seat's popular 850 saloon, for instance, was a doppelganger for the 1964 Fiat 850 with its rear-mounted 843cc four-cylinder engine. Seat's edition arrived two years later, adopting the Fiat 850 Special-tune 37bhp engine and four-speed manual transmission only, the Fiat clutch-less, torque-converter-activated semi-automatic being denied the Spanish market. With a 77mph top whack, the car felt more agile than its 0–62mph figure of thirty-three seconds suggested, and it cost very little to run, although overheating was sometimes an issue because of a sticking thermostat.

Seat needed a specific four-door model to suit local tastes, and so produced its own with a 15cm-longer wheelbase and called it the Largo. Next it added some panache to its range with, in 1967, its own locally made version of Fiat's 850 Coupé with a more zingy 47bhp engine. And then, to round out what had become Spain's widest single range of cars, in 1969 it added its own edition of the Fiat 850 Spider.

Two things were unusual about this. For starters, it was going to be a niche model, and so the body panels in this case were imported directly from the Bertone coachworks in Turin; Bertone not only built the car there but had also designed it for Fiat, yet another mini-masterpiece from the pen and imagination of rising star Giorgetto Giugiaro. Secondly, Fiat had trademark claim to the word 'Spider', so Seat's car was named simply 850 Sport.

They shared an identical engine. This was a 903cc 52bhp unit, with a longer stroke, Weber/Bressel 30 DIC 1 two-body carburettor and 9.5:1 compression ratio, and an alternator instead of a dynamo. It could manage a frantic 93mph – even though fast roads were hard to find in Spain at the time, apart from in Catalonia – and ran wider radial tyres on a slightly increased track. Lower rear suspension than the 850 Coupé gave more negative camber, improving roadholding, although the rear engine position always demanded respect. It was a light car, weighing just 705kg (1,554lb), with the neat little optional hardtop adding only another 10kg (22lb).

The 850 Sport was rare, with a mere 1,746 assembled until 1972. Compare that to 100,000 other Seat 850s on average each year and you can see its impact was vanishingly small. Fiat forbade any non-Spanish sales, so there were no exports. All Italian and Spanish 850s were heading for history at this point because the front-wheel drive Fiat 127, and related Seat 127, were superseding them. The Fiat 850 Spider was replaced by the mid-engined Fiat X1/9, and Spain never had its own version of that. The Seat 850 Sport, meanwhile, has become a coveted jewel of the marque's heritage but still its only ever convertible.

1969 PININFARINA FERRARI 512S

Rounding out an epic decade for Italian car design was this fantastic example of the art created around a Ferrari 512S racecar chassis. It's probably the most extreme of all the 'wedges' of the period, the work of Pininfarina's Filippo Sapino and first seen in Turin in October 1969, although sadly it was never a running car.

1969 TOYOTA EX-III

At the Tokyo motor show in November 1969, the Japanese finally cottoned on to the benefit of the show car as eye candy, with Toyota eager to prove it could match Bertone and Pininfarina for wild and impractical styling, with a little pseudo-science thrown in. That 'glasshouse', for sure, showed originality.

Volvo 142.

Audi Super 90.

Citroën 2CV Sahara.